MAJOR VOICES
IN
AMERICAN THEOLOGY

MAJOR VOICES
IN
AMERICAN
THEOLOGY

Six Contemporary Leaders

by

DAVID WESLEY SOPER

Professor and Chairman of the Department of Religion
Beloit College, Beloit, Wisconsin

KENNIKAT PRESS/PORT WASHINGTON, N. Y.

MAJOR VOICES IN AMERICAN THEOLOGY

ESSAY AND GENERAL LITERATURE INDEX REPRINT SERIES

*Every woman is a theologian, and two have
taught me — my mother and my wife*

Contents

Introduction

To men hungry for meaning, theology is bread, for men cannot live by morality and mechanism alone. We cannot do without science, and science cannot do without us. Meaning and morality cannot do without science, and science cannot do without meaning and morality. Similarly, we cannot do without the social sciences, and they cannot do without us. Neither science nor social science has failed man; it is man who has failed them. Again, we cannot do without the humanities, as the humanities could not have been without us. Without meaning, which is every man's ultimate concern, neither morals nor mechanism can survive. For the question must and will be asked: What is the meaning of morals and mechanism? If no meaning exists, what is the meaning of science, of ethics, and of literature?

In greater or lesser degree all men are theologians, for man is precisely the question about meaning—his own meaning, and the meaning of every thing around him, the meaning of nature and history, of science and literature.

But questions are not answers. We have tried to live by questions, and have become spiritual starvelings. If there is no ultimate answer, we will invent our own; indeed, we have endlessly invented the false answers: the worship of race, of proletariat, of property, of national sovereignty, the worship of man the question rather than of God the answer. To live without God is to substitute mammon for meaning.

Not only is theology bread to men hungry for meaning, but it is also pure water and strong wine to men athirst in the Sahara of modern meaninglessness. This is the age of hunger and thirst for meaning. Men are weary and bored with questions regarded as answers. In this age particularly, theology must either " put up or shut up." If it has an answer, that answer must be translated into twentieth century speech. Without meaning, man's achievements are one with Nineveh and Tyre. Modern man faces two alternatives: meaning or madness. Theology must speak not merely about the meaning which man creates, but primarily about the meaning and the mystery which have created, and are now creating, man.

The hunger of meaninglessness for meaning — this accurately describes our stormy century. To this hunger this book is intended to speak. To men without hunger this book has nothing to say. There are many other important voices in contemporary theology: at a later time we hope to give them sustained attention.

The six men here presented were not arbitrarily chosen. Seminary presidents and deans, professors of systematic, exegetical, apologetic, dogmatic, historical, and philosophical theology, and leaders from many Protestant denominations were asked in detail and at length for their suggestions. Twenty-four contemporary American theologians were nominated. Of the twenty-four, these six headed every list.

The sequence of chapters is in no sense a scale of importance. The reader will make his own value estimates. To this writer, one study seemed the best commentary on its predecessor, and the best introduction to its successor. Continuity of idea and discontinuity of treatment determined the order of presentation. Personal inclination and interest, it goes without saying, could not be wholly eliminated.

Each theologian has been read with admiration and affection; each is, in his own right, a treasury of merit. Each chapter presents one modern master — first in biography and book sequence, second in careful examination of characteristic ideas. Every chapter has been forwarded to the theologian studied to be checked for errors of fact. Where suggestions have been made, they have been incorporated. The six men are not to be held to account for the following pages. Each treatment, as such treatments always are, is a portrait, not a photograph. Every effort, with care and love, has been put forth to make each chapter something more than a caricature. It is obvious, nonetheless, that the following pages present these men, in exposition, in appreciation, and in criticism, as one contemporary sees them: no less, and no more.

Four years ago, in conversation, Nels F. S. Ferré urged me to prepare a readable book on contemporary American theology. I answered very simply: " There is no American theology." My own study, since 1939, had been exclusively preoccupied with European theologians, ancient, medieval, and modern. In 1947, 1948, and 1950 I completed a series of personal interviews, on the meaning and message of basic theology for this age, with thirty-three major European thinkers, from Rome to Edinburgh, from Geneva to Oxford, and from Paris to Prague. My reply to Ferré was sincere: I felt then that American theology was still in its adolescence.

A year and a half ago, again in conversation, Ferré reopened the subject; he stressed the need of a thorough but readable story, with essential content, of contemporary theology in America. A lively correspondence followed with The Westminster Press, and the project was under way. I am now convinced that contemporary American theology is not only of age but has something to say, something that needs saying, something that needs hearing, and something that modern meaninglessness is hungry to hear. The subject is not academic. There is very little of the ivory tower here. The subject is as practical as the bread and the breath of life. For meaning and mystery are exactly our daily necessities.

DAVID WESLEY SOPER

Beloit College
September 16, 1952

MAJOR VOICES
IN
AMERICAN THEOLOGY

THE HUMAN,
THE DIVINE,
AND THE DEMONIC

The Evangelical Theology of Edwin Lewis

The Evangelical Theology
of
Edwin Lewis

At an interview in Rome, Jacques Maritain said to me: "American Protestantism, in my opinion, needs two things: an intellectual rediscovery of Christianity, and a recovery of what the Quakers used to call 'the Inner Light.'" At many American seminaries — in particular at Drew University's graduate school of theology — he added, there was a genuine awareness of these needs and an intelligent attempt to meet them. Maritain has thus described with high accuracy Edwin Lewis' twin objectives, and, for those who have rubbed minds with him, his achievement.

It is often said that Lewis was first a liberal, then an evangelical, and is now a simon-pure Zoroastrian (one who believes that the battle between God and Satan is eternal). There is conspicuous truth, and falsehood, in the statement. During the skeptical twenties he was, for many, liberals, the chief spokesman, yet even then he was more, much more, than a liberal. If a modernist is one who discards essential elements in historic Christianity, the modernists, as Lynn Harold Hough put it, "failed to see that a more historic position than their own was implicit in his thinking" (*The Teachers of Drew,* edited by James Richard Joy, p. 144. Drew University, 1942). Similarly when Lewis became the leader of his majesty's loyal opposition, his conservative brethren failed to see the " implicit liberalism in his forceful dialectic for classical Christianity " (*Ibid.*). *The Manchester Guardian* correctly stated, "He is not a timid obscurantist but a Christian scholar who knows what science and philosophy are saying." Hough added, " The most microscopic scholar who tried to catch him napping would have a bad experience " (*Ibid.,* pp. 144, 145).

Of importance to all men in general, and to Drew men in particular, is the alleged irreconcilable controversy between Lewis and Hough. But the general practitioners have declared prematurely that there is war in heaven among the specialists. Deep and legitimate differences have been glorified as " the Battle of Drew Forest " or " the Battle of Missionary Ridge." It is often overlooked that Hough has always referred to Lewis as " an intimate comrade in the things of the mind " and a chief source of " the intellectual and spiritual accent which Drew men carry with them all about the world " (*Ibid.,* p. 145). Students of both professors, myself included, used to say: " We hear about God from Lewis, and about man from Hough, but we need all that we hear. They are a team of winged steeds; each offers what the other lacks." Hough once related the following story: Lewis had just delivered a powerful summons to evangelical recovery before a Methodist General Conference. A clergyman, laboring under the delusion that Hough and Lewis were bitter enemies, led Hough aside and whispered, " Well, how did you like that? " Hough at once replied, " One doesn't *like* the gospel; one *accepts* it! "

It was Hocking's *Layman's Missionary Report,* with its devaluation of Christ as God's supreme self-revelation, and Lewis' own editorial labor on *The Abingdon Bible Commentary* which drove him from evangelical liberalism to liberal evangelicalism, from philosophy to revelation. Documentary evidence exists that Lewis the Liberal and Lewis the Evangelical held common ground. *Jesus Christ and the Human Quest* (Abingdon-Cokesbury Press, 1924) stressed man's search for God; *A Christian Manifesto* (1934) accented God's search for man, but in both volumes faith and reason labored together as friends.

Fully as important as the upsweep from natural to supernatural religion has been Lewis' later downsweep from one world to three (*monism* to *pluralism*); he asserts three eternals, the creative, the discreative, and the noncreative, each self-existent. A careful reading of *The Creator and the Adversary* (1948) will disclose how significant is this change both to him and to us. Lewis has simply discovered that the battle between the divine and the demonic is no make-believe; it is tragically *real* in nature as well as in man. C. S. Lewis' *The Great Divorce* and *The Screwtape Letters* made the same point. Heaven and hell have been wedded blissfully in modern lack-of-thought: the two Lewises simply insist that God has put asunder what men have united. Lewis' new realism is moral as well as meta-physical. " Something has entered into his processes of interpretation," writes Hough, " which can only be called prophetic fire." The Church has often succumbed to sleeping sickness; drowsiness has often replaced vigilance. The alert have become the lethargic. These things have been lost to view: that the battle is *real,* that life is seri-ous, that it is possible to fail, that a choice for good and a choice for evil are not the same choice. Lewis brings the real war into sharp focus. He takes the soul's crisis (man's *existential dilemma*) out of academic moth balls. Dancing a monistic minuet may satisfy the false prophets; Amos, Jeremiah, and Edwin Lewis have recognized that the dance is the dance of death.

The thoughtful critic may have a mental reservation about Lewis' *eternal* pluralism. The critic may plead that the parallel lines meet in infinity, that the noncreative and the discreative are neither self-originating nor self-existent, that both receive their life from God, that the battle is all the more real because the devil is under a divine contract to destroy all that can be destroyed, to keep the whole of the divine creation under critical pressure. The critic may justly plead for one world *under* one God; nonetheless he cannot but sing a silent *Te Deum* that Lewis has reintroduced the theological " elderly maiden ladies " to the reality of the battle in nature and in man, the possibility of failure, and the necessity of the choice. " A man can get *damned* around here! "

The discovery, in succession, of the human, the divine, and the demonic — these are the three movements in Lewis' mind. But what about the man himself?

England was the land of his birth, April 18, 1881 — Newbury, about twenty miles from Oxford, to be precise. Lewis has often de-scribed with admiration his carpenter father's painstaking workmanship. An employer once said, " If all my men worked as you do, I'd be worth a million pounds." The good Lord may feel the same way about Edwin Lewis; he is everywhere recognized as a meticulous scholar. Lewis the elder believed that God, not man, was his workmaster. It seems likely that Lewis the younger similarly considers his assignment as solely from heaven.

At nineteen, Edwin Lewis came to Canada. He devoted four years to the Newfoundland Methodist Conference as a missionary, six years to the North Dakota Conference, although most of this time he was left without appointment to attend school, and nine to the Troy Conference. January 5, 1904, he married Louise Newhook Frost; there have been five children after the flesh, and ten thousand after the spirit — of whom I am one.

He was a student at Mt. Allison University in Canada, Middlebury College in Vermont, and the United Free Church College in Glasgow, Scotland. He received the A.B. degree at New York State College for Teachers in 1915, the B.D. (1908) and the Th.D. (1918) at Drew, and the D.D. at Dickinson in 1926.

He became a naturalized American citizen in 1916, and the same year served as English instructor at New York State College for Teachers in Albany. Two events of supreme importance occurred in 1916: Woodrow Wilson was re-elected, and Edwin Lewis began his long career at Drew. As instructor in Greek and theology he assisted Dr. Olin A. Curtis. When Curtis' health failed, Lewis carried on in his place. From 1918 to 1920 he was adjunct professor of systematic theology, then full professor until 1929; since that time he has been professor also of the philosophy of religion.

He was a delegate to the Methodist General Conference in 1928, 1932, and 1936. He is a Republican, but still able to breathe. He has lectured everywhere to clergymen, college professors, and human beings. A few years ago, circling the globe, he found his own graduates on every continent laboring creatively in the Spirit of Christ, carrying forward with distinction his own intellectual and spiritual ministry. For thirty-five years Drew students, and readers everywhere, have felt the thrust of his thought. Not a few of his students began their studies as belligerent atheists. I was a member of this fraternity.

Lewis once remarked, "I have seen many a young man through the intellectual measles." His 1951 retirement only releases him for a wider ministry. A student recently wrote with pardonable idolatry, "As far as I am concerned, it is not Edwin Lewis that is retiring, but Drew University."

But now to the movement of his mind.

THE SEEKING MAN

Lewis first came to public attention with *Jesus Christ and the Human Quest*. The book was well named, for the entire volume is preoccupied with man's search after God. At this point in Lewis' experience the seeking God has not as yet become visible. Note the words, "It makes no difference whether God is conceived as a self-sufficient being wholly distinct from man, or whether he is conceived as nothing more than a necessary constituent of human consciousness" (P. 63). The context discloses that man, a pursuer of objectives in the mind, cannot escape an inner compulsion to seek after God. Whether or not God exists *outside* the mind, he does exist *inside;* he is real enough to the God-intoxicated. All religious activity begins with man. "The life-process is a process of self-realization, determined solely from within, although contingent on the nature of external conditions. . . . Man is fundamentally a seeker of ends" (P. 38).

The motif of man-centered religion is continued in *A Manual of Christian Beliefs* (1927), is modified by the discovery of a reality greater than man in *God and Ourselves* (1931), but is still dominant in *Great Christian Teachings* (1933). It must not be denied, however, that a secondary motif of God-centered religion exists from the first. God seems but a junior partner in the human enterprise, but he is increasingly granted executive authority. One receives a distinct impression that Lewis may have been a vigorous theist from the beginning, but intimidated by a hostile climate of opinion. Faith seems ashamed of itself. It may have been his desire to make the gospel acceptable to the strongest of the skeptics, and on their own ground. Nor was he wrong in his apparent idea that to assert the reality of a transcendent God would mean his quick classification, and dismissal, as a Fundamentalist. He wanted the skeptics to hear what he had to say, and he knew they could be persuaded to listen only on their own terms. Faith does appear to have its back to the wall in the Lewis of the twenties; it is even fighting for its life. Everyone who lived through that arid decade will remember that Walter Lippmann's *A Preface to Morals,* with its sad stoicism in a meaningless world, seemed as high as the mind could go toward a supernatural faith. There were Fundamentalists and atheists and nothing much between. Fundamentalists had turned their backs upon secular science, and atheists were Fundamentalists turned inside out. The *fun* and the *damn* were evident in Fundamentalism, but not the *mentalism.* An educated believer in that dismal day had to walk an intellectual tightrope to escape a damning classification, and a " Fundamentalist " was less acceptable than an " atheist " among the " intelligentsia." Lewis was not an atheist, though I remember hearing him called one, yet he dared not make a noise like a Fundamentalist.

In any case, a dimension of transcendence is traceable all the way. Even in *Jesus Christ and the Human Quest* you have the telltale assertion, " God became man in order to accomplish a necessary human deliverance " (P. 272). You have there also the recognition that Christ himself, the total Person, is the revelation of God, and the realization that in the Saviour's agony on the cross sin accomplished its worst but sounded its own death knell; thus disclosing its true nature, it made possible both repentance and forgiveness. There is more than a hint of Augustine in the idea that man is meant for God, and short of God he is not wholly man.

It is possible, and seems probable, that the pre-*Manifesto* Lewis had not resolved a contradiction in his thinking. Faith may have been struggling not so much for expression, or even for existence, but for coherence. A complete structure of thought and faith, particularly a mature Christian theology, is not the work of a day — or a decade. There were seeds of supernaturalism in the earliest Lewis, and they were growing on productive ground, but they had fallen among thorns. In *A Manual of Christian Beliefs,* Lewis leaves, if only momentarily, the seeking man for the seeking God; he asserts that there must be in God a capacity for man corresponding to man's capacity for God. Jesus is presented as a human life continuous inwardly with God and outwardly with history; he appears human only, yet he is not alone a man of his time, but also a man of no time. We are assured that God is purposive yet approachable, suffering yet all-sufficient, holy yet humbly incarnate in human flesh; nevertheless he remains more amiable than active. The activity is still in man.

Lewis did the greater part of the editorial work on *The Abingdon Bible Commentary* (1929); he himself contributed the two articles on " The Miracles of the New Testament " and " The New Testament and Christian Doctrine." These studies gave little comfort to the liberals but less to the literalists. At this point many a young theologian reluctantly reclassified every miracle as myth, though with a clearer understanding he need not have done so. In Lewis' argument, Christ himself is the greatest miracle; in the light of who and what he was the lesser miracles are not incredible. Lewis even insisted that the Christ of the New Testament cannot be explained on a purely naturalistic basis. God was in Christ, and the New Testament is the realm of the supernatural where language, forced out of contact with the natural, could go but haltingly. The New Testament, precisely because it is an anthology of early Christian literature, clearly depicts the life and faith of the Church. The Community of Christians grew through faith and love centered in Jesus Christ conceived as divinely sent Saviour, and through surrender to the control of the Spirit. Lewis expresses his mature views on Biblical interpretation and illustrates his methods in detail in *The Biblical Faith and Christian Freedom* (The Westminster Press, 1953). Looking back on the Lewis of *The Commentary* from the sixth decade of this negative century, he seems but mildly modernistic and substantially available to all classical Christians. Man still holds the limelight, but he is ad-libbing his lines; God plays only a supporting role, but the play is his, and he wrote it, and he is moving downstage.

God and Ourselves insists that God is real, that he is greater than man and greater than the world, that he is the meaning of all things, but the argument struggles stubbornly in the Nessus shirt of an apologetic spirit. It is a polemic, not a song. To whom must one apologize for faith? *Great Christian Teachings,* if not the least, is the last of Lewis the Liberal. It pleads, piously enough, that Christian holiness means Christlikeness, the greatest thing in the world, but implies that the supreme good is attainable without the deep surgery of divine grace. When Jesus said his Kingdom was " not of the world," he meant only that it was not the kind of Kingdom with which the world of his time was familiar.

But Lewis, the prince of the Liberals, is not to be remembered merely as a theologian of the seeking man; he was also, and remains, a theologian of the social conscience. He was as responsible as any-one else for the truth of the honorable, and dubious, tribute that Methodism and the " social gospel " were two terms for the same thing. Though Lewis later moves from man to God, the theologian of social responsibility remains. At no time does Lewis find escape from this world through the discovery of another. From first to last he summons the Church to social reconstruction in the love of Christ. In *The Creator and the Adversary* you still have the down-to-earth realism of *A Manual of Christian Beliefs,* which contains the following statement:

" The possibility of a universal cataclysm in which civilization shall destroy itself grows every day more real. What can save mankind from perishing of its own achievements? One thing only — the enthronement of Jesus Christ as King of Kings and Lord of Lords.

" But such an enthronement will not be a merely negative thing. Christ will not simply stave off ruin: he will bring a positive salvation. If he could have his way with men, there would be no industrial oppression, no hopeless little children, no cheerless old age, no grinding poverty, no fattening of the few on the toil of the many, no racial hatreds, no arma-ments, no false standards of judgment as between man and man. Only as the race can make progress in this direction can there be any hope of the future, and such progress depends entirely on whether or not the follow-ers of Jesus Christ are willing to leave the eternal fate of their souls in their Lord's hands while they devote themselves to the task of making his Spirit operative in the world of today " (P. 130. Charles Scribner's Sons, 1927).

LEWIS AND BARTH

In American theology the early 1930's constituted a watershed be-tween predepression naturalism and postdepression supernaturalism.

Prosperity gave way to prophecy. The City of God was rediscovered beneath the City of Mammon. The imponderable logic of economic chaos undoubtedly had much to do with it, but the new climate of opinion is traceable also, if not primarily, to a European source. Whatever American theologians finally conclude about the Calvin after Calvin, it is obvious that he stabbed liberalism awake. The Kierkegaard after Kierkegaard proved a Christian Socrates, a God-intoxicated gadfly disturbing all man-centered religion. The Bönn bomber talked as though God has the audacity to exist; further, that precious little of importance exists beside him. God is a good deal more than man's aspiration after the ideal; he is the Initiator and the Goal of man's spiritual activity. From beginning to end, God is the *totaliter aliter,* the totally other. Thus did Barth appear in 1933.

The *Layman's Missionary Report* on the one hand and Barth on the other heightened Lewis' dissatisfaction with effeminate liberalism and deepened his awareness of God the Almighty. One must not, however, conclude that Lewis is in any sense a European echo. No more definitive criticism has ever been written than the third of Lewis' three articles on Barth in *The Christian Century* (1933). Lewis precisely delineated the major flaws in Barthianism. In the first place no absolute cleavage between God and man can be said to exist. If mutual exclusiveness is granted, God can no longer be called "Father." Lewis nonetheless applauds Barth's all-out attack upon historicism and psychologism, the one padlocking the deity behind the prison bars of time, the other imprisoning him within the processes of the mind. Liberalism had narrowed the gulf between holy God and sinful man; God had been humanized and man deified; but Barth had widened the chasm beyond all reason. To Lewis, the God who is forever beyond is also the God who is already within. But for God below, man could never reach out for God above. God, who is always on the offensive, moves toward a man inherently approachable and able to respond. It is God who seeks, but he is also sought. Some kinship between divinity and humanity exists.

In the second place Lewis attacked Barth's authoritarianism. On Barth's terms, God has spoken to mankind through the men of the Bible, but nowhere else. We are asked to believe solely on the prophetic and apostolic testimony. We are required to accept the Word of God wholly on the word of man. Lewis insists in rebuttal that to know God only at second hand is not to know him at all. A capacity to receive the divine revelation must have existed within the Biblical writers; if a similar capacity does not exist in us, we can never understand their words. The Holy Spirit conceived the New Testament in the womb of the Church. Granted! But the same Spirit may, and must, conceive in us.

A third devastating criticism is specifically Christological. Barth presents a docetic Christ, and thus robs us of Jesus. To Barth, even Christ's resurrection is not to be understood as historical, lest it partake of the futility of the temporal. Fundamentalists have had trouble with Barth on this point. In Barthianism the Jesus of history has given way entirely to the Christ of eternity. Jesus has ceased to be that Christ might be. Lewis inquires, " What should we know of ' the Eternal Christ' but for the historical Jesus? " (" Where Is Barth Wrong? " *The Christian Century,* March 22, 1933, p. 386). True, the question may legitimately be turned around. What indeed should we know of the historical Jesus but for the spiritual Christ? It is through the Church and the Spirit that our knowledge of Jesus has come. Still, it is precisely this knowledge that we refuse to surrender.

The Barthian flaws are obvious and glaring. No one can afford to hurry over them. Nonetheless Lewis makes us hear the prophet's own accent. He that has ears to hear, let him hear. Let every man take what he can use, and use what he takes. The world is not God, and God is not the world, though but for God the world could not be. Man *is* dead; only God can make him live. The Infinite and finite stand in absolute contrast, and the gulf between the two can be bridged only from the divine side.

Barth underestimated the values of liberalism, but has rendered conspicuous service in casting away its vices. As a student of Herrmann and Harnack, he had absorbed from youth the standard doctrines of German liberalism — that the Bible records man's progressing thoughts about God, that God is immanent in nature, history, and humanity, that man is by nature a son of God, that Jesus Christ supremely illustrated this sonship, that every man can, by faith and

love, realize his oneness with God. Neither the divine Sacrifice nor
the divine Sovereignty are essential. Barth learned in ten years as a
pastor the futility of these themes. Barth discovered that man's
search for God always ends in failure; precisely this search and this
failure characterize all religion. Over against religion, which attempts to bridge the gulf from man's side, is Revelation, which
bridges the gulf from God's side. This Revelation is Jesus Christ.

Barth is no Fundamentalist. He desires, not less critical scholarship, but more insight. The textual critic stops at the threshold of
the real task — to interpret what God has said. Revelation is a divine
invasion, not a human achievement. The religion of the natural man
who fails to find God is one thing; the religion of the man whom
God has found is another.

Though Barth has created an absolute cleavage between God and
man where none exists, though he has established a new authoritarianism which must be transcended, though he has taken away
Jesus for the greater glory of Christ and must give him back again,
still one may say with Edwin Lewis:

" Sitting at the feet of Karl Barth, we are brought to confess with deep
sorrow that modern liberal theology has lightly parted with much precious treasure. It threw overboard what it thought was useless rubbish
and now sees was the cargo. Barth is offering a vicarious penitence for
the sins of the modernists, the humanists, the psychologists, the religio-
historicists, and all that ilk. Small wonder that the burden he has assumed
well nigh crushes him, and that there goes up from his soul the cry of
dereliction. If only the thieves would consent to be crucified with him! "
(*Ibid.*, p. 387).

The Seeking God

Since *A Christian Manifesto*, the liberals have regarded Lewis with
that peculiar dislike reserved for traitors to the cause. They know
full well that he is in no sense a Fundamentalist; they are aware
that he has asserted from first to last that literalism is a perversion
of Protestantism, that the Bible exists as an instrument of the Spirit
to confront men with God, that the Word which came by the Spirit
can only be apprehended by the Spirit. Lewis' enemies are not unaware that he has never been a Fundamentalist, yet they have so

classified him in the vain hope of driving him from the field. They have succeeded in part. Many who are on Lewis' side in the controversy, some of them his own disciples, have denied or betrayed him in public, fearing to be bracketed with the Biblicists. Such is the price of leadership. On the whole, however, the prophets of Baal have reckoned without Elijah. Lewis increases — he does not diminish — with the years.

A major need in our time, in any time, is a term accurately representing the classical Christianity which is always modern without modernism and fundamental without fundamentalism. No adequate term exists or is likely to, for the departures from Christianity are easier to label and much easier to publicize. To begin with, they possess the garish color which characterizes extremes; they can be seen, even by laymen, from a distance. The central tradition, faith and reason laboring together with love, is harder to discern; it has neither superficial sparkle nor provincial prejudice. It is not an isolated community, remote from civilization; it is civilization. It is not a county, to be visited or neglected at will; it is a continent where freedom and authority dwell together in peace.

With *A Christian Manifesto, The Faith We Declare* (1939), and *A Philosophy of the Christian Revelation* (1940) Lewis the Evangelical transcended Lewis the Liberal; he is visible at full maturity. Once for all the point has been driven home that theological liberalism, at bottom, was nothing more than an attempt to unite philosophical naturalism and Christianity without benefit of clergy. The attempt was doomed to failure from the start, for naturalism in philosophy and Christianity are implacable enemies. Christianity is the religion of the supernatural: that is, it is *really* a religion, not a meaningful ethic in a meaningless world. Lewis traces the attempted illicit union between Christ and Belial to Hegel. All his defense of spiritual reality notwithstanding, Hegel's imposing philosophy was in effect only an all-inclusive naturalism that had signed a treaty of perfect and perpetual peace with scientific determinism. Hegel's God could not *do* anything. Reality is too many-sided to be compressed into a Hegelian strait jacket; life breaks through logic; Samson breathes deeply and snaps the Philistines' shackles.

Lewis is a bitter disappointment to Fundamentalists and Modernists alike when he insists that Biblical myths are not meant to be true, but to symbolize truth. What is alone important is the apprehension of the creative idea. As Lewis sees it, it is better to take the difficult passages in the most literal sense, if only on this condition they are meaningful, than by taking them otherwise to lose their meaning.

The Christ of the New Testament summons us to discipleship — on his terms, not ours. No one who says that he believes in Jesus but does not believe in God ought ever to regard himself as a Christian. Utterly alien alike to the spirit and the letter of Christianity is that form of liberalism which announces its belief in Jesus, and at the same time renounces its belief in that God but for whom Jesus himself could not have been.

Recently a typical American liberal announced publicly: " Christianity is anything anybody says it is." Edwin Lewis holds a different view. If the Christian faith, as such, is not to perish from the earth, the Church in our time must rediscover, asserts Lewis, that Christianity is not the collected absence of identifying characteristics; rather, Christianity is forever identifiable as *belief,* as *experience,* and as *a way of life.* It is the *belief* that God, of whom and through whom are all things, at infinite self-cost did in Jesus Christ manifest and satisfy his holy love, thereby making an atonement for the sins of the world and opening a way to forgiveness and reconciliation. As *experience,* Christianity is the realization of sins forgiven; the knowledge of God reconciled; the sense of peace within; a sure confidence in the face of the ills of life; an inner awareness of the presence and favor of the Lord; a satisfaction in the fellowship of those who share Christ's name and spirit; and the possession of an increasing passion for souls. As *a way of life,* Christianity is behavior consistent with the purpose to glorify Christ and exhibit him before the world. It is Christlikeness, love beyond suffering, compassion making sacrifice of self; it is the realistic endeavor to make every life, every relationship, every institution, an incarnation of the will of God, that in all things Jesus Christ, who is the image of the invisible Father, " might have the preeminence."

In Lewis the Evangelical there is no longer an apologetic spirit; he asserts that Christianity as Revelation is unequivocally true. Jesus Christ is more than the apex of man's pyramid of ideals. Though he is not the totality of the Godhead, the totality of the Godhead is in Jesus Christ self-revealed. The Son discloses the Father, and the Spirit makes Father and Son real to the believer. Christ is the meaning of God, of man, and of history.

The Church calls the sons of men to become the sons of God; but more, it offers men in the Holy Spirit the power to respond to the call. Only a Church greatly believing will be greatly achieving. When the gospel of the Spirit has been neglected, the Church has become feeble and futile; nothing but the spiritual gospel has ever brought it back to power. Always must the Word become flesh; always must the Church rediscover the Spirit.

Lewis the ex-Liberal has gained new insight into human evil; something in man neutralizes and betrays his loftiest aspirations. If God must make his way into human life by human means, the means may, and does, immeasurably hinder him. There is a kingdom of evil and man holds membership in it. Satan must be cast out of the heart if he is to be cast out of history. Lewis the theologian is so well known that Lewis the social philosopher has been lost to view. In *A New Heaven and a New Earth* (1941) Lewis presents the specifically Christian foundation for an ecumenical society. A new earth always awaits a new heaven; a new actual always awaits a new ideal; the new production always awaits the new pattern. The Society that is the Trinity provides the only basis for the brotherhood of man. On any showing an increase of fellowship is the one criterion of a new and better earth. The great and terrible Day of the Lord is that day when God pours out upon men his Spirit in a fashion never before known. On that day, " whosoever shall call upon the name of the Lord shall be saved." *This is the Day!* So declared the Church on the Day of Pentecost. Put in mundane terms: to what extent we can ever have an entirely Christian social order is a question, but it is no question that we can have a better one.

Lewis is a mature philosopher and theologian; he has thought through, as few men have done, the meaning of the Christian Rev-

elation. But he is always also a preacher under the skin. Pulpit practitioners, in England as well as America, have secured a full barrel
of sermons per book from the " Christianity-at-the-clergyman's-
level " volumes which are Lewis' later production. In *Christian Truth
for Christian Living* (1942), *The Practice of the Christian Life*
(1942), and *The Ministry of the Holy Spirit* (1944) Lewis the active parson's brain trust is at his best. Even the wayfaring man,
though a layman, can read these books with profit. Two ideas domi-
nate these slender books (can any book be too slender for the mimeo-
graph minister?): (1) To say that there is no fundamental difference in the Christian's relation to God and his neighbor from what
is possible to one who is not a Christian is simply to say that Jesus
Christ has had no profound and revolutionary effect upon the world.
(2) Heaven is wherever the Spirit of Christ is in complete possession. Wherever he is granted full control, the heavenly pervades the
earthly. In Lewis' words:

" In a very real sense, the incarnation was ' miracle. It was not simply
something that a man was doing: rather, it was something that God himself was doing. That is why we call it an incarnation.

"Pentecost may very well be regarded as a second 'miracle.' . . .
Shall we call it the completion of the meaning and the purpose of the
incarnation? That day, a great new reality burst upon the world. . . .

" All that God himself is, all that he would do for men, all that he
would suffer that his will might come to pass, has been set forth in Jesus
Christ. Here are human souls that believe this, that believe it without any
hesitation, that yield themselves completely to it — *and that is why the
Holy Spirit can move in upon them as he does.* . . . That benediction
which falls upon the praying soul is the Holy Spirit crowning a movement of the soul which he himself originated " (*The Ministry of the
Holy Spirit*, pp. 21, 82, 127. Tidings).

THE BATTLE OF GOD

A third movement had already begun in the mind of Lewis before
The Creator and the Adversary. The central idea was present in
A New Heaven and a New Earth, but exactly expressed in *The
Practice of the Christian Life*:

" No man can think very long about life and its purposes without finding himself compelled to face the fact of evil. . . . In whichever direc-

tion he may look, he sees that which he is not able to call good. . . . It is to a large extent our human nature itself which is the source of the evil we have to fight. The temptation to pride, vainglory, laxity, ambition, various forms of indulgence, and the like, do not depend on where we happen to be. God has an enemy, an enemy whom he must overcome if his ultimate purposes are to be fulfilled " (Pp. 93-96. The Westminster Press, 1942).

This fact of experience becomes in Lewis' major work, *The Creator and the Adversary,* a complete metaphysical system. All things, Lewis argues, arise through the opposition of darkness and light; the creativity of God, working upon chaos, seeks endlessly to overcome discreative resistance. The idea of a real war between good and evil, with casualties on both sides, is neither new nor revolutionary. With varying emphasis you will find it in every major mind since Paul. For sophisticated moderns, what is new about Lewis' argument is its absolute and uncompromising dualism; for his three eternals, the creative, the discreative, and the noncreative, are morally but two; that is, the noncreative is neutral by definition.

To Lewis, once you dispose of the adversary as the source of all resistance to the love of God, on any grounds whatever, or allow him status as a secret partner in the divine enterprise, you have lost Biblical realism; the battle in which you cannot but choose sides is without hope of armistice. The God of holy love has reckoned, and must reckon *forever,* with the bitter opposition of the adversary. The *dark resistance* penetrates deeper than the will of man. It goes down to the very roots of existence. Man's misuse of freedom is but one bitter fruit on the tree — an effect, not a first cause.

Determined resistance to divine activity is a common idea from Plato onward. In our time it has received an intriguing variety of treatments. Brightman places the resistance within God himself — hence the term " finite " applied to the deity. Evil is a kind of cosmic ache within the divine abdomen; God is as baffled by it as we are, but is laboring heroically, and hopelessly, to cure it. The chief criticism of the view is obvious; it makes God no more and no less than an enormously large man — proportionately no better equipped than man to overcome evil. Lewis' deity is finite also, but the resistance is wholly outside, not inside God, outside him from all eternity, and quite as old as he, yet passive and powerless until God creates. Satan cannot create; he can only destroy. Until there is something to destroy he might as well be nonexistent. God initiated the conflict by initiating creation. Further, on Lewis' terms, God is able to throw into the conflict sufficient resources to turn defeat into victory. Nels Ferré insists that all the world's dark evil, from cancer to earthquake, is the activity of Agape, the vigilance of sovereign love, whose purpose to bring every soul through freedom to fellowship cannot and will not be denied. Man chooses his way with freedom; he is free even to disobey and defy God. But God holds all the honor count; he controls the board and can overplay or trump any card man chooses to lead. Every man will eventually see that God's will is best. In this incarnation, or the thousandth to come, every soul will be saved. The Ferré optimism solves many problems, but creates as many as it solves. It restores sovereignty to God the Almighty and brings everything under control; you have one world instead of two. The chief criticism is evident: universal salvation is clearly alien to the mundane realism of the New Testament; on that older view, it is possible to be *lost* permanently. Sentimentality, however disguised, seems to be, and is, peering over Ferré's shoulder. Lewis' view has at least no softness; it is no siren song. It does not make the monistic mistake of modifying the distinction between good and evil; it does not underestimate the reality and the tragedy of evil. It relieves God of the split personality with which Brightman endowed him; it deprives man of Ferré's certainty of salvation. A stimulating insecurity accompanies the soul's pilgrimage. As some humorist put it, " There is no security in numbers, or in anything else." The battle is real; the master choice will stand eternally, and only unconditional surrender is acceptable in heaven. The chief criticism of Lewis' split universe is clear: it denies the divine origin of the noncreative and the discreative; Satan is " used " to keep the whole creation under critical attack, but was not " created " to do so. The serious critic may contend that Satan was specifically created to occupy his place on the divine payroll, that his task in the cosmic economy is to break every handiwork of God that can be broken. God wills man's salvation, as an artist wills that every work of art shall be a masterpiece, but God is also the absolute critic of his art; he wills the destruction of all that can be destroyed, all that lacks the integrity and the vitality to survive. Man's role in the drama is desperately, breath-takingly real. His master choice is decisive; there is no in-between; he either hastens or thwarts his own completion as a divine handiwork. Satan cannot destroy the elect (who love God because he first loved them), but he can, and must, put them to the test. The winds of adversity demolish every house on sand, but strengthen every house on rock. Man must make his peace with God the Creator and Redeemer, or he will have to deal with God the Destroyer.

In any absolute dualism hope is an orphan; it finds no place to lay its head. But Lewis' dualism is not as absolute as it seems; he is, after all, a Christian first, and a dualist second; he insists upon the reality of hope.

" It is not to be denied that by his very act of creation, God gives the adversary his opportunity, and that evil and sin become an inevitable concomitant of the creative act. It is not to be denied that God permits evil to run its course, since he can halt it only by halting everything else, and that is to admit final defeat. It is not to be denied that God makes use of evil in many a subtle way to further his own purpose of good, not doing evil that good might come, but enduring evil that good might come. . . . All is not merrily right with the world simply because God's in his heaven. Much is wrong with the world, God in heaven notwithstanding. But it is still true that because God *is* in his heaven — better still, because God does not *stay* in his heaven, as one ' sitting apart, contemplating all,' but enters the arena of conflict as a personal participant, most present, like a faithful leader, where the strife is fiercest — because this is so, it is the assurance that *not all is wrong with the world,* and that it may more and more become right " (*The Creator and the Adversary,* p. 152. Abingdon-Cokesbury Press, 1948).

In Lewis' view, God initiates by his creative act the divine-demonic conflict, but is not to be held responsible for originating either the noncreative or the discreative. At this point the inadequacy of the " finite " God becomes apparent. By his creative act God gives the noncreative and the discreative their significance, but is not the source of their existence. This leaves the origin of the noncreative and the discreative entirely unexplained. The *ex nihilo* theory insists simply that the noncreative and the discreative are not self-explanatory; on Lewis' view they are self-explanatory; that is, they " exist because they exist." No one will deny their existence, and few will deny that their " meaning " is given them by God, but many will justly question whether their " existence " is self-explanatory.

Lewis is not primarily interested in a neat metaphysical system; his first interest is the reality of the battle between the Creator and the adversary, and the Creator's final victory. His view is essentially that of Martin Luther, as Reinhold Niebuhr has quoted and interpreted him:

" Luther, less philosophical than Calvin and more prophetic in temper, preserved the essential paradox more successfully. To him the devil was ' God's Devil.' God used him to his own ends. ' Devil,' declares God in Luther's words, ' thou art a murderer and a criminal, but I will use thee for whatsoever I will. Thou shalt be the dung with which I will fertilize my lovely vineyard. I will and can use thee in my work on my vines. . . . Therefore thou mayst hack, cut, and destroy, but no further than I permit ' " (*An Interpretation of Christian Ethics,* p. 75. Harper & Brothers, 1935).

The thoughtful critic may or may not reject Lewis' split infinity, but he cannot fail to stand up and cheer Lewis' ethical seriousness. As Niebuhr sees it, " it is better for religion to forgo perfect metaphysical consistency for the sake of moral potency. In a sense religion is always forced to choose between an adequate metaphysics and an adequate ethics " (*Does Civilization Need Religion?,* p. 214. The Macmillan Company, 1927). In any case, *The Creator and the Adversary* is a trumpet with certain sound summoning the Christian to recover his faith, and the Church its gospel. Creation is creativity in perpetual strife with discreativity, and, on any terms, the battle is as real as Christ's cross.

To every Christian life is a daily call to love, but discreativity attacks him most often and most effectively through discouragement. The greatest, and the rarest, virtue is simply patience. " Wait on the Lord " said the psalmist again and again. Restless moderns may well heed Lewis' similar words.

" *This* place, *this* task, *this* moment, contains the possibility of a divine revelation to the soul. From what spot may a ladder reach up to heaven? From that stone there at your very feet. . . . The narrow limits to which you are confined by a will not your own may be another Patmos. . . . To be ' in the Spirit ' on *any* day makes that ' the Lord's Day ' indeed " (*The Ministry of the Holy Spirit*, p. 116).

THE INSUFFICIENCY
OF
MAN

The Critical Theology of Reinhold Niebuhr

The Critical Theology
of
Reinhold Niebuhr

A lone pioneer, Reinhold Niebuhr broke through the Modernist-Fundamentalist wilderness of the first third of this century and established a base of operations for subsequent explorers. To use a different figure, personal and social Christianity were at war; Niebuhr has made possible something more than an armistice: he has mobilized the former enemies in a common crusade — to lead our sub-Christian century to contrition and new venture. He has performed the prophet's task of criticism.

Every thoroughgoing critic is bound to be the center of a storm of controversy. Two groups in the main continually attack Niebuhr: on the one hand, those who feel that his view of the sinfulness and partiality of all human achievement paralyzes all human effort, and, on the other, those who are perhaps too certain that his emphasis not only accents the insufficiency of man, but also, in effect, the insufficiency of God. Archbishop William Temple summarized the attack from the left in his well-known Limerick, written shortly after Niebuhr had completed a series of lectures in England:

> "At Stanwyck, when Niebuhr had quit it,
> Said a young man: 'At last I have hit it;
> Since I cannot do right
> I must find out tonight
> The best sin to commit — and commit it.'"

It is overlooked in this attack that in all his books Niebuhr continually stresses the necessity of action in this world toward the best approximation of virtue in the soul and equal justice in society, that he endlessly asserts that the humility which recognizes the persistence of sinful self-love on the highest level of achievement in no way destroys moral ardor; it simply destroys self-righteousness and false pretense. It is also overlooked that he perpetually criticizes Barthian theology for its failure to perceive the necessity and value of proximate solutions to difficult problems in this relative world. It is true that he takes liberalism to task for its lighthearted dismissal of the sinfulness of man and the transcendence of God. But with equal persistence he takes orthodoxy to task for its neglect of this world in its preoccupation with the next.

The attack from the right insists that Niebuhr overestimates forgiveness and underestimates fellowship; that he does not see that repentance, necessary though it is, is not the end but the means to the end. True, the broken heart is the only entrance to the Kingdom, not alone at the beginning of the Christian pilgrimage, but every day, and as much at the end as the beginning. Yet the nature of the Kingdom is mutual love, between God and the soul, and between the soul and society; the agape fellowship is the end, forgiveness the means. Intentionally or not, Niebuhr leaves you with the reverse impression.

Niebuhr was fully aware of these opposite attacks from the start. In the wholly delightful *Leaves from the Notebook of a Tamed Cynic* there is this diary entry:

"If I do not watch myself I will regard all who make their adjustments to my right as fanatics and all who make them to the left as cowards. . . .

"A reasonable person adjusts his moral goal somewhere between Christ and Aristotle, between an ethic of love and an ethic of moderation. I hope there is more of Christ than of Aristotle in my position. But I would not be too sure of it. . . .

"It is almost impossible to be sane and Christian at the same time, and on the whole I have been more sane than Christian" (Pp. 166, 167, 195. Willett, Clark & Colby, 1929).

Niebuhr's chief significance lies in the fact that he has reunited theology and history in holy, and productive, wedlock. These whom

God had joined together, and man had put asunder, he has made one again, and the marriage is recorded in heaven. But what of his life and hard times?

After the manner of man, he was born, June 21, 1892, at Wright City, Missouri. He is still "from Missouri" and can never quite be shown. His father was Gustave Niebuhr, a scholarly German preacher, who died when the children were young, but not before he had taught Reinhold "that the critical faculty can be united with a reverent spirit." It was not an easy task for the mother, Lydia (Hosto) Niebuhr, to assume the complex responsibilities of her children's nurture. Helmut Richard Niebuhr, two years Reinhold's junior, has made his own record and his own distinguished contribution to American thought. The mother later served as Reinhold's assistant pastor for twelve years in Detroit.

A brief glance at Niebuhr's boyhood suggests his strong Lutheran conditioning, and discloses as well his later reinterpretation of the relation between ultimate security and temporal insecurity. In his own words:

"The need of security is a basic need of human life. I remember how wonderful was the experience of my boyhood when we ran to the barn, warned by ominous clouds of an approaching storm, and then heard the wind and the rain beating outside while safe and dry under the eaves of the haymow. The experience had actual religious overtones. The safety and shelter of the haymow were somehow symbolic of all security against dark and tempestuous powers. The words of the psalmist committed to memory in confirmation class, achieved a sudden and vivid relevance: 'Thou shalt not be afraid for the terror by night; nor for the arrow that flieth by day; nor for the pestilence that walketh in darkness; nor for the destruction that wasteth at noonday. . . . There shall no evil befall thee, neither shall any plague come nigh thy dwelling.' This word of the psalm is, incidentally, a perfect illustration of all the illusions which may arise from an ultimate religious faith. When faith in an ultimate security is couched in symbolic expressions which suggest protection from all immediate perils, it is easy to be tempted to the illusion that the child of God will be accorded special protection from the capricious forces of the natural world or special immunity from the vindictive passions of angry men. Any such faith is bound to suffer disillusionment. Nor does it deserve moral respect" (*Beyond Tragedy,* pp. 96, 97. Charles Scribner's Sons, 1938).

This may be too lighthearted a dismissal of the persistent idea of special providence; Niebuhr believes in both general and special revelation and therefore has no effective argument against both general and special providence. Nonetheless, this retrospection reveals much of his youth, and of his maturity.

Reinhold and Richard Niebuhr attended Elmhurst College in Illinois (now of the Evangelical and Reformed Church). In 1910, Reinhold left Elmhurst without a degree to enroll in Eden Theological Seminary in St. Louis, then of the Evangelical Church, now Evangelical and Reformed. He transferred from Eden to Yale in 1913, and there received the B.D. (1914) and the M.A. (1915). The same year he was ordained by the Evangelical Synod of North America and began pastoral duties at Bethel Evangelical Church, an auto workers' congregation in Detroit. *Leaves from the Notebook of a Tamed Cynic,* by far the most readable of Niebuhr's books, is a penetrating, and at the same time hilarious, study of a young pastor's pilgrimage through the school of hard knocks. Actually the book contains most of the insights that characterize the mature Niebuhr, yet mixes profound introspection with a delightful play-by-play account of the grandeur and misery of life in church and industrial community. He was keenly interested in ethics and dubious about theology, yet some transcendence is evident on every page. He was unwilling to entertain great moral ideas without attempting to realize them in life and society, and equally unwilling to proclaim them in abstract terms without bringing them into juxtaposition with the specific social and moral issues of the day. He despised the cheap scolds, and the sentimentalists, among his fellow ministers, and slowly developed his unique critical gift. His method is clear, from beginning to end, in these words from his 1920 diary:

" The real meaning of the gospel is in conflict with most of the customs and attitudes of our day at so many places that there is adventure in the Christian message, even if you only play around with its ideas in a conventional world. I can't say that I have done anything in my life to dramatize the conflict between the gospel and the world. But I find it increasingly interesting to set the two in juxtaposition at least in my mind and in the minds of others. And of course ideas may finally lead to action " (P. 27).

It is obvious that "playing around" with the conflict between the gospel and the world not only became "increasingly interesting" but finally the master passion. He defined religion as a reaction to life's mysteries and a reverence before the infinitudes of the universe. He recognized, however, that without ethical application religion might never come to grips with tragedy. The soul both reverently and morally vital could apprehend the infinite in terms of holiness, and worship a God transcending both human knowledge and human virtue.

During these years he was much more than a critic of the depersonalized society produced, along with automobiles, by Detroit industry. He was also, and perhaps primarily, a critic of himself. Note these words from the diary of 1924:

"A spiritual leader who has too many illusions is useless. One who has lost his illusions about mankind and retains his illusions about himself is insufferable. Let the process of disillusionment continue until the self is included. At that point, of course, only religion can save from the enervation of despair. But it is at that point that true religion is born" (P. 91).

The small working-class church grew in size and grace; presently a new building was required and obtained. Sunday evening forums centered discussion on critical social issues — attracting intellectuals, radicals, and liberals of every shade of opinion. Sessions were sprightly, and sometimes explosive. There among Detroit factory workers Reinhold Niebuhr developed his profound sympathy for the proletariat. He became the doughty David of the disinherited against every Philistine Goliath. He once said, "The lowliest peasant of the Dark Ages had more opportunity for self-expression than the highest paid employee in the Ford factory." Had he been a pastor of the privileged, his point of view undoubtedly would have developed differently — to our loss. As it was, the bitterness of the workers against their exploitation and depersonalization by the factory system became his own.

Angry words in the *Notebook* denounce Ford's millions held in reserve while workers starved. The Marxian faith in the worker as the future savior of society entered into his soul.

Socially conservative church circles considered Niebuhr dangerous, and did not realize how dangerous he was. There were flare-ups
between Niebuhr and Detroit employers. In 1928 he left Detroit, not
without reluctance, for mutual love had grown between the shepherd
and his flock; the *Notebook* acknowledges the strength their occasional heights and depths of faith had given him. He entered the
comparative quiet harbor of Union Theological Seminary in New
York City, as associate professor of philosophy of religion. Since
1930, he has been professor of applied Christianity. He was no less a
social radical at Union. He blended conservative Lutheran and Reformed theology; the political philosophy of John Dewey, whose
naïve faith in "free inquiry" he later rejected; the economic approach of Karl Marx, whose utopianism became apparent to him,
but whose perception of the "ideological taint" in all bourgeois
thinking he continued to value; and the everyday intricacies of the
American labor movement. During the depression of the thirties he
rose to commanding influence in the theological world. He confirmed Americans' suspicion that something was radically wrong
with society, and suggested a revaluation of all values as the first
deep surgery.

Early journeys to postwar Europe, particularly to postwar Germany, convinced Niebuhr that his earlier antipacifism needed revision. For a time he espoused tentatively the pacifist cause. In 1932,
with *Moral Man and Immoral Society,* he broke completely with
pacifism, considering it a utopian miscarriage of social responsibility,
issuing from a sentimentalized view of God and man. Necessary
social change — for example, from a bourgeois to a proletarian society
— could be accomplished only by force. He was fully aware that religion, in particular medieval and Reformation Christianity, had been
as much a liability as an asset in social reconstruction, and developed
this dual view in the book *The Contribution of Religion to Social
Work* (1932), the 1930 Forbes Lectures at the New York School of
Social Work. With *Reflections on the End of an Era* (1934), he pronounced the doom of capitalist society. He visited strikers, talked to
unions, and entered wholeheartedly into the activities of the Socialist
Party. For a time he was editor of the Party paper, *The World To-*

morrow. With *Christianity and Power Politics* (1940), Niebuhr had discovered, and dispelled, his utopian illusions. He was considerably less certain what might lie on the other side of social breakdown; he no longer lightly hoped for the collapse of a social system which continued to offer a degree of freedom, and with it the possibility of achieving better social and economic adjustments. Hope of breakdown was only feasible when any alternative was preferable to an existing tyranny. Undoubtedly three well-known personalities had something to do with the change in Niebuhr's emphasis. Franklin D. Roosevelt's attempt to bring economic power under social control, whether failure or success, ameliorated working-class hatred of capitalist society; and the rise of Mussolini and Hitler indicated to many a sensitive conscience that a contest of power between freedom and tyranny was not far away.

Every man is both imbedded in the society of which he is a part, and transcends it. The break with the Socialist Party was inevitable. Niebuhr himself tells the story, and the reasons behind it.

"A letter from the Socialist Party informs me that my views on foreign affairs violate the Party platform and asks me to give account of my nonconformity. The Party position is that this war is a clash of rival imperialisms in which nothing significant is at stake. . . . I answer the Socialist communication by a quick resignation from the Party. . . .

"'There is not much difference between people,' said a farmer to William James, 'but what difference there is is very important.' . . .

"Utopianism creates confusion in politics by measuring all significant historical distinctions against purely ideal perspectives and blinding the eye to differences which may be matters of life and death in a specific instance" (*Christianity and Power Politics*, pp. 167–169. Charles Scribner's Sons, 1940).

Long before December, 1941, Niebuhr was the leader of a group of eminent churchmen who believed that war could be a lesser evil than tyranny; together they denounced the immorality and irresponsibility of isolation. February 7, 1941, the group presented to the public the first issue of *Christianity and Crisis*, an eight-page biweekly opposed to the stanchly pacifist tone of existing denominational periodicals, in particular of *The Christian Century*. The magazine was dedicated to the principle that "the halting of totali-

tarian aggression is a prerequisite to world peace and order." Bishop
Ivan Lee Holt, Bishop Francis J. McConnell, President Dodds of
Princeton, William Allan Neilson, former president of Smith College, and many others gave the paper their backing. Antipacifist
churchmen were given a thorough hearing. Churchmen who remained pacifist, Niebuhr and his group believed, were guilty of a
sentimentalized Christianity which preferred slavery to war. Consciously or not, the pacifist was on the side of tyranny; since resistance to tyranny is war, tyranny is peace.

Niebuhr was the fifth American to deliver the Gifford Lectures.
His predecessors were William James, Josiah Royce, John Dewey,
and William E. Hocking. The lectures were given at the University
of Edinburgh in 1939, and published in two volumes, *Human Nature*
(1941) and *Human Destiny* (1943); they are now available in one
edition. Niebuhr's fresh approach to old controversies, his sharp
logic, and his theological brilliance penetrated the presuppositions
and pretensions of every alternative to the gospel of judgment and
redemption. Niebuhr argues that man is a paradox of finiteness and
freedom, that his sin issues not from his finiteness but his unwillingness to accept it, his excessive self-love, which produces defiance on
the one hand and fanaticism on the other. Mysticism sought falsely
to save man from impulse, and romanticism from reason. Prophetic
religion disclosed God the Judge who stands over against the partiality and idolatry in all human achievement; the Gospels disclosed
God the Redeemer who meets repentance with pardon, and com-
pletes in grace what man cannot complete in nature and history. It
is impossible for the reader not to be stirred to self-examination or
rebuttal. Niebuhr is often criticized for his severity, but surely he is
too severely criticized, for the surgeon must cut deeply before healing can begin. He is said to be too clever, and in greater need of
tenderness and compassion. After listening to him, one clergyman
remarked, " He can skin civilization, hang the hide up to dry, and
offer prayer over the carcass." His students, and thousands who not
having seen have believed, have responded affirmatively to his message, and consider him the lesser of two evils in contemporary theology. A gospel that underestimates the problem is always a greater

hazard than a criticism that underestimates the gospel.

It is of special interest that Niebuhr is not unaware of his hyper-critical temper. *Leaves from the Notebook of a Tamed Cynic* contains the following entry:

" I have been profoundly impressed by the Spenglerian thesis that culture is destroyed by the spirit of sophistication and I am beginning to suspect that I belong to the forces of decadence in which sophistication is at work. I have my eye too much upon the limitations of contemporary religious life and institutions; I always see the absurdities and irrationalities in which narrow types of religion issue. . . .

"I don't want anyone to be more cynical than I am. I can't justify myself in my perilous position except by the observation that the business of being sophisticated and naïve, critical and religious, at one and the same time is as difficult as it is necessary, and only a few are able to achieve the balance. H—— [probably Lynn Harold Hough] says I lack a proper appreciation of the mystical values in religion. That is probably the root of the matter. Yet I can't resist another word in self-defense. The modern world is so full of bunkum that it is difficult to attempt honesty in it without an undue emphasis upon the critical faculty " (Pp. 132, 133).

There are, in reality, two Reinhold Niebuhrs, if not more. On the one side he is the fearless and honest critic of our age, and of the ages that have preceded ours; with exact scrutiny he weighs the Middle Ages along with Reformation and post-Reformation and finds them wanting. On the other side, he is a messenger of good news, a bearer of the gospel. This side of Niebuhr is the lesser side. He seems considerably more a John the Baptist than a Saint John. Perhaps he that is least in the Kingdom of Love is greater than he. He himself apparently had something of the kind in mind when he wrote in his Detroit diary: " I am not really a Christian. . . . I am too cautious to be a Christian " (P. 166). He is more of an Amos than a Jeremiah. Amos prophesied doom for Israel as Niebuhr has prophesied doom for our liberal bourgeois culture. Jeremiah also prophesied doom, but wept over Judah as Christ wept over Jerusalem. The tears are not apparent in Niebuhr. Yet there is a strain of faith and love in him which is so rarely apparent that it is a special delight. Even in his first book, *Does Civilization Need Religion?*, though Niebuhr the critic is evident, there is more of positive faith and love than in many a later work. Christianity seems often a principle of criticism rather than a song of love and joy. Yet some of the later works, perhaps because they were addresses given on college campuses, accent the positive gospel. *Beyond Tragedy* and *Discerning the Signs of the Times* (1946) are not only more readable than the heavier books, but also contain something more than criticial attack on an age which has substituted departure from for approximation of the Christian faith. New Testament peace and joy shine through these pages. They offer healing as well as surgery. Yet *An Interpretation of Christian Ethics, The Children of Light and the Children of Darkness* (1944), and *Faith and History* (1949) return to the business of thoroughgoing criticism: the first of the absence of transcendence in liberalism, and the absence of immanence in orthodoxy; the second of the false optimism of bourgeois democracy, yet the necessity of democratic freedom; and the third of the various views that assume that history is redemptive, that time will solve all the problems.

The critical theology of Niebuhr will always need the postcritical theology of Nels F. S. Ferré to complete it, and vice versa. Niebuhr himself appreciates, whether or not he is able fully to achieve, childlikeness. These words from *Faith and History* sound more like Ferré than Niebuhr:

" There is, of course, no easy road from maturity back to childhood. A too simple return to the innocency of childhood results in obscurantism in the realm of culture and social primitivism in the realm of man's moral life. Yet the return is both possible and necessary.
" The way to it lies in a wisdom which recognizes the limits of human knowledge and a humility which knows the limits of all human powers " (P. 54. Charles Scribner's Sons, 1949).

Clearly this is Saint Paul's " I know in part," and something other than the pride that makes each thinker consider himself the final surrogate for God. Notwithstanding the constant Niebuhr criticism of literalism in religion, he has a word of appreciation for the evangelistic cults which somehow succeed in shattering the self in repentance as a prelude to power, however serious their fault in deriding reason and ignoring social justice.

He has by no means confined himself to the professor's chair and the lecturer's platform. He has headed the Union for Democratic Action; has served as chairman of American Friends of German Freedom. As editor of the quarterly *Christianity and Society,* he has demonstrated the unique relevance of "applied Christianity" to the stubborn conflicts of our century. Journals too numerous to mention have published his articles and clamored for more. He is a contributing editor of *The Christian Century* which he once attacked as the voice of effeminate liberalism. *The American Scholar, The Christian Century, Newsweek, Time,* and many other leading magazines have discussed him repeatedly and at length, though as often with acidity as with benevolence. Many a doctoral dissertation has painfully elaborated his ideas, and many a book is now in preparation, or in print, offering a character or a caricature. It is safe to predict a long life to his influence.

The better colleges and universities have honored themselves and him with honorary degrees: Grinnell, Wesleyan, Pennsylvania, Amherst, Yale, Oxford, Harvard, Hobart, Occidental, Princeton, Glasgow, and New York. Obviously there will be others. Catholicism has often burned its critics at the stake; Protestantism prefers to kill its critics with kindness.

In 1931, Reinhold Niebuhr married a former student, the Englishwoman Ursula Keppel-Compton, and there are two children: Christopher Robert and Barbara Elizabeth. He may be seen with his family on the few afternoons when he is not encouraging or criticizing the saints in Europe or the American provinces, walking on Riverside Drive — his only recreation.

He seems "tall, bald, and cold," something of a theological owl looking out wisely, and unblinkingly, on the world. Yet there is warmth in him, and it is felt beneath the tumult and the shouting of his prophecy. His photographs suggest a Lutheran Voltaire without a periwig. He even resembles Calvin Coolidge, though he is considerably more committal, yet also "against sin."

His significance lies in the fact that his feet are firmly planted in history. He is not an ivory-tower philosopher, but from the first has dealt heroically with the intractable stuff of society, which always reduces every ideal to a mere approximation. There is stubborn inertia in all reality; existence offers determined resistance to creation. Each new step is inevitably a compromise between the creative will and the concrete world. History steadfastly defeats, and reveals, God.

Niebuhr is definitely in, but as definitely not of, the world. He has his eyes on the Absolute which appeared in Galilee; he expects and accepts conflict and refuses the cowardice of capitulation. He is aware that capitulation without conflict reduces religion to magic and secularizes life. Let the chips fall where they may, Niebuhr grapples wholeheartedly with nature and history. He understands that the cross was inspired by devotion to a "kingdom not of this world"; yet that the cross was also the method by which that Kingdom was changed from ethereal to concrete reality. Only the absolute, which is beyond history, moves men to defy and subdue the relative. Niebuhr realizes that a religion perfectly at home in the world offers no counsel which the world cannot gain from secular sources. The creative and redemptive struggle is real, but not hopeless. Religion preaches hope as well as repentance, and rescues men from despair as well as complacency. He understands the absurdity, and glory, of faith.

"Only the foolishness of faith knows how to assume the brotherhood of man and to create it by the help of the assumption. A religious ideal is always a little absurd because it insists on the truth of what ought to be true but is only partly true; it is however the ultimate wisdom, because reality slowly approaches the ideals which are implicit in its life. A merely realistic analysis of any given set of facts is therefore as dangerous as it is helpful. The creative and redemptive force is a faith which defies the real in the name of the ideal, and subdues it" (*Does Civilization Need Religion?*, pp. 44, 45).

THE INSUFFICIENCY OF MAN

Every prophet needs a decadent age, and vice versa. The critical faculty is a less desperate necessity in an age of growth. Without criticism a civilization moves toward disintegration without light and without hope. The prophet may not arrest the momentum of decay, but its nature could not be understood without him. Indeed, an articulate conscience in a conscienceless society is bound to leave some kind of mark, if only to point the way for future pilgrims. Undoubtedly conscience is in part a sociological product, yet conscience has always been " most perfectly expressed when men have defied the mediocre or perverse standards of a given community in the name of a religiously apprehended higher standard." Reinhold Niebuhr has offered precisely this defiance. He has unquestionably punctured the idolatrous pretensions of our culture, yet fully appreciated the periodic despair into which our complacent moralism, legalism, and rationalism have led us. In one sense he has been a psychological scientist; he has enabled us to analyze our true motives, to separate our published purposes from our actual desires; he has decreased hypocrisy and increased morality. He has destroyed the consistent confidence in human virtue which makes faith irrelevant, and has thereby made faith possible, though not inevitable. It is probably not too much to say that he has reintroduced conscience, and indeed Christianity, into Christendom.

He has succeeded primarily because he has understood, as few have done, that prophecy is applied theology. He has been content neither with a transcendence which neglects the world, nor with an immanence which neglects God. In his thinking the vertical and the horizontal meet. There are always a few prophets of the transcendent, and many prophets of the immanent. Niebuhr is perhaps the most articulate modern to unite the two perspectives, making each the critic of the other. This creative interplay is possible precisely because Niebuhr considers man an organic union of flesh and spirit.

" The soul and the body are one. . . . This unity of soul and body does not deny the human capacity for freedom. It does not reduce man to the processes of nature in which he stands, though yet he stands above them. It merely insists on the organic unity between the two. The mind of man never functions as if it were discarnate. That is, it is not only subject to the limitations of a finite perspective but also to the necessities of physical existence " (*Beyond Tragedy*, pp. 293, 294).

Theology and history are therefore in permanent and perplexing tension. The Christian doctrine, not of simple immortality, but of the resurrection of the body, in his view, emphasizes this organic unity; he finds it also the basis of social as over against merely in-

dividual religion. Niebuhr thinks with the Bible, though he inter-
prets it mythologically rather than literally; he considers sin, as does
the Bible, in both religious and moral dimensions. The religious
dimension of sin is rebellion against God, its moral and social dimension injustice. The self which prematurely makes itself the
center of existence inevitably seeks to subordinate other selves to its
will. Niebuhr's theological conservatism releases him from modern
sentimentality, and his social radicalism similarly releases him from
the this-worldly irresponsibility of the pious. Beyond all sin he perceives the possibility of the broken heart, and the healing of pardon
and power. He offers no false security, no security at all short of
divine grace, and he has the true prophet's courage to speak clearly
to the majority whether or not he is a minority of one. To the modern nontragic view of history he offers only tragedy. He places a
time bomb at the base of every Tower of Babel. Christian Church
and pagan State alike come to judgment. Proximate answers to perplexing questions, and proximate solutions to social problems, he
regards as perpetual necessities. Mixed with the humility which is
despair with faith, these proximate answers and solutions create the
difference between greater good and greater evil. Mixed with pride,
the proximate is mistaken for the ultimate, and secular defiance or
religious fanaticism produce the remorse which is despair without
faith. Beyond all tragedy, Niebuhr apprehends the divine love and
power which bear the whole human pilgrimage, shine through its
enigmas and antinomies, and are finally and definitively revealed in a
drama in which suffering love gains triumph over sin and death.

Man's predicament lies in the fact that the human problem is insoluble with human resources. Man is imbedded in nature, yet infinitely transcends nature. He is a paradox of finiteness and freedom.
His sin issues not from his finiteness, but his unwillingness to accept
it, his pride, his desire to make himself the center of the universe,
his will to make himself independent of God. Any view that accents
only the grandeur of man fails to account for his misery. Any view
that emphasizes only man's depravity fails to account for his awareness of it.

"Man is mortal. That is his fate. Man pretends not to be mortal. That is his sin. Man is a creature of time and place, whose perspectives and insights are invariably conditioned by his immediate circumstances. But man is not merely the prisoner of time and place. He touches the fringes of the eternal. He is not content to be merely American man, or Chinese man, or bourgeois man, or man of the twentieth century. He wants to be man. He is not content with his truth. He seeks *the* truth. His memory spans the ages in order that he may transcend his age. His restless mind seeks to understand the meaning of all cultures so that he may not be caught within the limitations of his own " (*Ibid.,* pp. 28, 29).

If man were totally depraved, he would not know that he is depraved, he would not seek endlessly to justify himself to himself, he would have no feeling of guilt, no uneasy conscience, no reaching out for the truth, beauty, and goodness which are always beyond his grasp. If he were totally depraved, he could neither desire nor receive the divine revelation; the stability and mercy at the heart of the universe would be beyond his comprehension. Because man is essentially good, yet always involved in sinful self-love, he is a perpetual contradiction. He seeks a divine grace not only greater than his sin, but greater also than his righteousness.

Man is torn between religious humility and sinful pride: this is his dilemma. From this situation man cannot extricate himself. The self that is to change itself is as troublesome as the self that is to be changed. No one can decide to be humble; the very decision establishes the self from whose dominion freedom is sought. Humility issues only from the heart that is broken at the foot of the cross, the heart that has seen, in the broken body of the Son of God, the meaning of its sin. No one can will a broken heart unless the wrath and the love of God have been revealed to him. In the knowledge that God is forever against sinful self-love, yet forever for the self, that God takes man's sin into his own heart and suffers it — only in this knowledge can the heart become humble.

Nature can be known through scientific inquiry, but scientific knowledge does not disclose its own meaning. The meaning of natural and human existence is disclosed from a trandscendent perspective available only to faith and love. The knowledge of God does not proceed from rational processes, though it eventually engages them. The knowledge of God is available only to the heart that is broken, and illumined, by the Holy Spirit.

" The Christian gospel as the final answer to the problems of both individual life and man's total history is not proved to be true by rational analysis. Its acceptance is an achievement of faith, being an apprehension of truth beyond the limits of reason. Such a faith must be grounded in repentance; for it presupposes a contrite recognition of the elements of pretension and false completion in all forms of human virtue, knowledge, and achievement. It is a gift of grace because neither the faith nor the repentance required for the knowledge of the true God, revealed in the cross and the resurrection, can be attained by taking thought. The self must lose itself to find itself in faith and repentance; but it does not find itself unless it be apprehended from beyond itself " (*Faith and History,* p. 151).

At the end of self, God. Rational process, with all its virtues, cannot apprehend him, for self-trust and self-assertion are always involved in self-analysis. The Renaissance idea of salvation by reason failed to take into account that it is precisely reason which turns the will-to-live into the will-to-power. Reason cannot find in itself a vantage point beyond self-interest. Marx discovered the ideological taint in all bourgeois morality. Bourgeois ideals were rationalized bourgeois interests. The sinful exploitation of the poor had been hidden behind the high-sounding pretense. But Marx failed to realize his own ideological taint, the rationalized envy of the proletariat. Reason is aware that it ought to be free, but is never as free as it ought to be. Lack of wisdom is not due primarily to a defect of the mind; it is due rather to a corruption of the heart; selfish pride introduces confusion into every historical conclusion. The human mind is so weak, so easily enslaved and prostituted by passion, that one is never certain whether the aristocratic fear of anarchy and revolution is an honest apprehension of evil or a dishonest attempt to take advantage of the proletariat. Reason not only justifies egoism, but endows it with a force it does not possess in subrational nature. Rationalism has no impartial perspective from which to view, and no transcendent fulcrum from which to affect, human action. Privileged groups have habitually denied the underprivileged every opportunity to cultivate innate capacity, and then ungallantly accused them of lacking what they had been denied the right to acquire.

Scientific investigation achieves relative impartiality as long as the object of its study is not an object of its desire, or as long as the facts it accumulates remain uninterpreted. As soon as meaning is added to measurement, presupposition destroys impartiality. The modern belief that scientific objectivity may be simply extended from nature to history obscures the unity of the self which acts, and is acted upon, in history. It also obscures the ambiguity of the self as both an effect, and a cause, of history. The self as creator does not master the self as creature merely by the extension of scientific know-how. The self is always an interested participant in every event, yet transcends itself enough to know that this is true. The common sense of mankind has always labeled as ridiculous every denial of human freedom, every evasion of human responsibility and guilt.

Man is a sinner, but he is more than a sinner because he is aware of his sin. Yet with his own resources of mind and will he cannot extricate himself from his dilemma. Because he is aware of his guilt, he transcends H. L. Mencken's cynical characterization: " Man is a sick fly taking a dizzy ride on a gigantic flywheel. . . . He is lazy, improvident, unclean. . . . Life is a combat between jackals and jackasses " (*Does Civilization Need Religion?, p. 40*). Precisely this cynicism characterized the Nazi view of non-Nordic man.

The modern assumption of self-sufficiency is nothing more than finiteness without humility.

" To be self-conscious is to see the self as a finite object separated from essential reality; but also related to it, or there could be no knowledge of separation. If this religious feeling is translated into moral terms it becomes the tension between the principle of love and the impulse of egoism; between the obligation to affirm the ultimate unity of life and the urge to establish the ego against all competing forms of life. . . . All modern moral theory may be briefly described as complacent finiteness " (*An Interpretation of Christian Ethics*, p. 67).

Essential Christianity and modern culture at this point are irreconcilable. The final conflict is between those who have a confidence in human virtue which human nature cannot support and those who have looked too deeply into human character to place their trust in so broken a reed.

THE INSUFFICIENCY OF HISTORY

Modern optimism, in contrast to Christianity's provisional pessimism, issues from the simple secular faith that history *is* Christ, that is, that history redeems itself. Christianity offers ultimate hope because its confidence is in the power and love of God; its provisional pessimism rises in its experience of human double-mindedness, its awareness that the highest idealism and the most hideous baseness exist side by side, and with all sincerity, in the same man, and even more in the same society. Human collectives, whether Churches or States, families or labor unions, are always more selfish than individuals. While Christianity seeks God's will on earth as in heaven, it has no naïve faith in any group's ability to transcend its own egoism.

Christianity's basic universalism dwarfs the provincial and partial perspectives of nations and cultures. Christianity comprehends the whole of history, and not only the story of a particular people; further, it deals with the problem of evil ultimately, and not merely from the standpoint of what may appear evil to an individual or a nation beset by competitors and foes. Christianity comprehends the whole of history because it is a religion of revelation; it knows by faith of certain events in history, in which the transcendent meaning of the whole panorama is disclosed. To Christianity, history is precisely a drama, not a mechanism of cause and effect which can be charted scientifically, not a sequence of inevitabilities which takes no account of freedom.

The secular faith, in history as itself redemptive, was clothed by liberal Christianity in traditional Christian phrases; the evolutionary process was the actual content of the liberal creed. Fundamentalism, on the other hand, sought prematurely to prove the truth of the Christian faith by denying and defying the fact of development in nature and history. The Christian concept of creation *ex nihilo* is not a denial of development; it simply insists that the temporal process is not self-explanatory.

The Christian view that history, either in whole or in part, cannot complete itself, has been wrongly used to justify cowardly resignation to known evils. Aware of creaturely limitation, religion has frequently prompted a defeatist attitude toward scientific efforts to ameliorate natural evils or social efforts to overcome historical evils. Yet this miscarriage of Christian humility is in contradiction to the Biblical faith, which always affirms the potential value of historical life. It was precisely *in* history, and not in a flight from history, that the divine love which suffers and sustains history was revealed. In contrast to every idolatrous culture, the divine revelation, which has manifested itself in history, cuts down everything that exalts itself against the knowledge of God. In short, the meaning of history transcends the historical process.

Fanaticism, whether religious or irreligious, whether Catholic or Communist, is simply the tendency within any economic class, any national or ecclesiastical hierarchy, to consider its partial perspective absolute, to consider itself God. Society is unable to complete itself, to save itself, precisely because egoism intrudes itself sinfully into all social achievement. Even the highest truth may be prostituted to the lowest purposes. The self-worship of individuals, and even more of nations and civilizations, expresses itself more plausibly in a truly universal religion than in any obvious idolatry. There is no absolute defense against the corruption of Christian truth through national or ecclesiastical pride and pretense. The sad history of Christian fanaticism proves that no version of the Christian faith has been immune to the error of claiming absolute significance for relative insights. Thus the Roman Church has uniformly sanctified medieval feudalism; thus Reformed Christianity has uniformly sanctified laissez-faire economics; and thus Marxism has uniformly sanctified the self-interest of the proletariat.

The fanatic fury of orthodox Marxism rises in its naïve faith that history is itself redemptive. The Marxian messianism endows a particular class in society with premature sanctity; its secular utopianism asserts the coming appearance, in history, of a kingdom of perfect righteousness (i.e., a classless society and an anarchistic brotherhood). Communism's absolute self-righteousness constitutes its real peril. The conventional objections to Marxist "materialism" and "atheism" are beside the point. Materialism is, on the whole, a justified reaction to purely otherworldly religions which do not understand that life is social and material as well as spiritual and moral. Marxist atheism is less deadly than Marxist idolatry. Orthodox Communism worships a god who is the unqualified ally of one class in society against all others.

The Christian view of life through death is applicable to individuals, but also, though more rarely, to nations. For example, Britain's absolute monarchy was forced to submit to constitutional limitation, and thus extended its life, thus found life through death. Precisely at the point of challenge by new forces, every political or social structure either resists and is destroyed, or submits to judgment and is renewed. No nation may achieve absolute justice within its borders; no society of nations may perfectly satisfy the legitimate aspirations of all its members; yet equal justice may always be more adequately approximated. Approximation becomes tragic departure, however, when the privileged class which controls the political system within a nation or the privileged nations within a society of states seek selfishly to maintain their position at the expense of the total community.

Naïve social scientists have assumed that men of power, and nations of power, will immediately curb their excessive demands upon society, as soon as they have been informed that their demands are antisocial. The egoistic corruption of individuals, and even more of nations, is wholly underestimated. All moralists, whether religious or rational, fail to comprehend the brutal behavior of every human collective; the power and persistence of group pride is insufficiently grasped. Only relative justice is possible in the affairs of men, and the possibility always transcends actual achievement, yet relative justice inevitably requires something more than mere good will.

" Though educators ever since the eighteenth century have given themselves to the fond illusion that justice through voluntary co-operation waited only upon a more universal or a more adequate educational enterprise, there is good reason to believe that the sentiments of benevolence and social good will will never be so sure or powerful, and rational capacity to consider the rights and needs of others in fair competition with our own will never be so fully developed, as to create the possibility of the anarchistic millennium which is the social utopia, either explicit or implicit, of all intellectual or religious moralists.

" All social co-operation on a larger scale than the most intimate social group requires a measure of coercion. While no state can maintain its unity purely by coercion, neither can it preserve itself without coercion " (*Moral Man and Immoral Society*, p. 3. Charles Scribner's Sons, 1932).

Niebuhr asserts a simple social law: the larger the group, the stronger its egoism in, and against, the total community. This excessive self-interest necessitates a measure of countercoercion. Niebuhr finds the rational moralists wrong in their assumption that violence is intrinsically immoral. In Kant's view, nothing is intrinsically immoral except ill will, and nothing intrinsically good except good will. Yet if violence is to be justified at all, as surgery to check cancerous growth, it must be applied with the surgeon's skill and with the surgeon's healing purpose. Indeed, nonviolence itself is a form of coercion. Negative resistance does not achieve spirituality simply because it is negative; it may express ill will as readily, or more readily, than good will. As long as it enters the field of society and places physical restraints upon the desires and activities of others, it is a form of physical coercion.

In Niebuhr's view, Christianity must usually side with the poor against the privileged, and with democracy against tyranny; as he sees it, society is always a contest of power, and the competing powers are never equally good or equally evil. Since equal justice is the only acceptable objective for society, social conflict which aims at greater equality has a moral basis not found in efforts which seek the perpetuation of privilege. War for the emancipation of nation, race, or class, is different in kind from war for the perpetuation of imperial rule or class dominance.

Niebuhr believes that democracy, to survive, must be divorced from its traditional defense. Democracy must and can have a stronger foundation than bourgeois optimism and individualism, now in need of revision. Man's capacity for justice, says Niebuhr, makes democracy possible; but man's inclination to injustice makes democracy necessary. The will to survival becomes, through the misuse of reason, the will to power, imperialism, and domination. To rest democracy's case upon human self-sufficiency is to rest it upon a false dogma; in Christian thought, self-sufficiency is recognized as the primal sin. Self-love, the root of all sin, takes two social forms: the domination of other life by the self, and isolationism, which is irresponsibility. Yet democracy is necessary, because its system of checks and balances curbs the egoism of competing groups, each by itself seeking to establish a new tyranny. Democracy is necessary, because its insistence upon free criticism is a simple recognition that all historical reality, whether of Church or Government, whether of wise man or specialist, is involved in the flux and relativity of human existence, is subject to error and sin, and exaggerates its errors and sins when they are immune to criticism.

Some kind of communal life is possible upon this planet, but the world community must be built by men and nations sufficiently mature to understand that relative justice is achieved, not merely by destroying, but also by deflecting, beguiling, and harnessing inevitable self-interest and by seeking the greatest possible common ground between self-interest and the general welfare. Leading nations and men must be humble enough to understand that the self-interest to be deflected is not exclusively in the opponent or competitor; it is also in the self, individual or collective, even in the idealist who erroneously imagines himself above the battle.

Only faith in a transcendent as well as immanent God can view without final despair the personal and collective egoisms which obstruct human brotherhood. Because modern man has faith neither in divine transcendence nor in divine immanence, the tragic realities of human existence and human nature drive him to total despair; for this reason he grasps at a straw, and clings desperately to the false dogma of human goodness. Thus his actual virtue becomes vice, and his noble strength an ignoble shortcoming (*The Irony of American History,* Charles Scribner's Sons, 1952). Christianity believes in a divine mercy that overcomes the contradictions of human history, which man can never completely overcome on any level of achievement. But Christianity is embarrassed by the fact that the majority of modern Christians, particularly in America, have no other faith than modern secularists.

"The Christian faith finds the final clue to the meaning of life and history in the Christ whose goodness is at once the virtue which man ought to, but does not, achieve in history, and the revelation of a divine mercy which understands and resolves the perpetual contradiction in which history is involved, even on the highest reaches of human achievement. From the standpoint of such a faith it is possible to deal with the ultimate social problem of human history: the creation of community in world dimensions. The insistence of the Christian faith that the love of Christ is the final norm of human existence must express itself socially in unwillingness to stop short of the whole human community in expressing our sense of moral responsibility for the life and welfare of others. The understanding of the Christian faith that the highest achievements of human life are infected with sinful corruption will help men to be prepared for new corruptions on the level of world community which drive simpler idealists to despair" (*The Children of Light and the Children of Darkness,* p. 188).

THE INSUFFICIENCY OF THE CHURCH

Ideally the Christian Community is "the saving remnant" which offers healing as well as diagnosis to sub-Christian nations, cultures, classes, and persons. It summons to renewal through repentance without the false belief that any nation or person can fulfill the meaning and purpose of history. But alas, the Church as a historical enterprise is human as well as divine, and seldom approximates the ideal. The true Church, never identical with the Church visible, is precisely that community of saints, known and unknown, among whom life is constantly transformed because it is always under the divine word. But the Church that men experience from century to century in history is often as far short of saintliness as the secular world. Indeed, secularism may be basically no more than a healthy reaction against the premature maturity of the pious. The underproduction of saints curses Church and State alike.

Niebuhr became keenly aware of the departure of organized religion from its own avowed faith during the years immediately preceding our participation in World War II. Spiritual insight and moral sensitivity, in his view, had at that time sunk to a new low.

In an age of world tragedy, surrounded by the miserable victims of tyranny and conflict, organized Christianity had identified the slogan, "Keep America out of War!" with the Christian gospel. In 1940 he wrote:

"Modern Christian and secular perfectionism, which places a premium upon nonparticipation in conflict, is a very sentimentalized version of the Christian faith and is at variance with the profoundest insights of the Christian religion. . . .

"The 'liberal culture' of modern bourgeois civilization has simply and sentimentally transmuted the suprahistorical ideals of perfection of the gospel into simple historical possibilities. In consequence it defines the good man and the good nation as the man and nation which avoid conflict. . . . It is unable to make significant distinctions between tyranny and freedom because it can find no democracy pure enough to deserve its devotion. . . . It is unable to distinguish between the peace of capitulation to tyranny and the peace of the Kingdom of God. It does not realize that its effort to make the peace of the Kingdom of God into a simple historical possibility must inevitably result in placing a premium upon surrender to evil, because the alternative course involves men and nations in conflict, or runs the risk, at least, of involving them in conflict.

"This kind of perfectionism is bad religion, however much it may claim the authority of the Sermon on the Mount. . . . It is bad politics and . . . helps to make the democratic nations weak and irresolute before a resolute and terrible foe" (*Christianity and Power Politics,* pp. ix–xi).

In simplest terms Niebuhr is convinced that religion can survive in modern civilization only by divine grace; humanly speaking, religion is dying in Western culture for two reasons: it has not made room in its authentic faith for scientific fact, and it has not made its ethical resources available for the solution of social problems.

In particular, modern religion has failed to rescue the economic world from essential irreligion. Adam Smith replaced Thomas Aquinas as the moral authority of the businessman, and, the fulminations of the early reformers notwithstanding, Protestantism sanctified laissez-faire economics and accepted a divided world; vast areas of life were withdrawn not only from religious inspiration but also from ethical examination. Thus was created our present world in which "business is business" and "politics is politics"; the nonmoral character of two basic human relationships is taken for granted. "Business is business," "ethics is ethics," and never the twain shall meet.

The Church has injured itself needlessly, and endlessly, by its premature identification of medieval science with Christian revelation. The whole evolutionary controversy, in Niebuhr's view, was charged with nonscientific and nonobjective factors on both sides. In the one case the heretics sought a premature escape from the unique responsibilities of human freedom; and in the other case the orthodox sought a premature escape from human creatureliness. Neither saints nor sinners knew as much as they advertised. A religion which claims to know too much is guilty of idolatrous pride; it is also an expression of the will-to-power. Secular skepticism is, or can be, faith's path to purity. Modern science was wrong in its premature identification of external description with ultimate meaning, but fundamentalism was equally wrong in regarding transcendent meaning as an adequate description of natural sequence. Theology became a bad science and science a bad theology. The conscious and pious motive of secularism, whatever its unconscious and more sinful motive, was to remove the strait jacket which pseudo-Christianity had placed upon man. "Publicans and sinners" have often rescued an important truth, and restored wholesomeness in human relations, against the fanaticism of the saints, who had forgotten that sainthood is corrupted whenever either perfect knowledge or pure virtue is claimed as a simple possession. The antichrist of the righteous, on the long view, is more deadly than the antichrist of the sinners.

Yet the Church has rightly sought to protect divine and human freedom from the dissolving determinism of science. Science, as often as religion, is corrupted by its assumption that its relative knowledge is absolute. The modern distaste for the religious sense of guilt has frequently led modern culture to deny the idea of moral responsibility. Modern culture has placed all its eggs in the basket of the scientific method; and no scientific description of a moral act can ever disclose the area of freedom in which alternate choices are weighed. Scientific description is both external and retrospective. In its view, every act is determined by previous acts in an endless chain of cause and effect. To an external observer no conscious choice of good or evil is discernible.

The Church has failed to render its required and essential service to the cause of social justice. An inevitable vice of a really profound religion is its frequent indifference, and irresponsibility, toward the immediate problems of relative justice in human relations. When statesmen are judged, it must be remembered that the statesman must, and the prophet need not, consider the limitations of human society. The self-righteousness of the prophet in his quick condemnation of the statesman has obscured both ethical faith and political good works.

The cultural crisis of Western civilization issues directly from its substitution of secular religions for the Christian faith. German nationalism was the cheapest, and costliest, ersatz religion. But a messianic class, the Communist alternative, is as evil as a messianic nation; indeed in Russia the two have become one. Undoubtedly the working class enjoys a special historical destiny. But without a transcendent reference it cannot criticize its own mission; inevitably it imagines itself to be God, even if it does not believe in God — or perhaps particularly if it does not believe in God.

But the insufficiency of the Church is evident not alone in its relation to secular science and idolatrous religion. Interior problems illustrate abundantly that organized piety has more often preached than practiced its gospel of love. The evangelical dismemberment of the body of Christ has demonstrated the human tendency to consider every partial truth ultimate. There is a religious solution to the problem of religious diversity. Religious and cultural diversity are possible in a free society, without the loss of religious depth. The solution requires a high form of religious commitment. It demands that each religion, or each version of a single faith, proclaim its highest insights while yet preserving a contrite recognition that all creeds are subject to human corruption. Such a recognition makes tolerance possible and denies any religious or cultural movement the right to claim official validity or to demand an official monopoly.

There is a positive element in our resistance to necessary change that is evil precisely because it is spiritual. World Christian fellowship is obstructed by countless premature maturities. Lower and narrower loyalties stand against nobler and wider loyalties, and their strength lies not alone in natural inertia, but also in guile of spirit. Stubborn provincialism is as destructive as idolatry, and is idolatry. It is obvious that religion has both created, and prevented, world community in State and Church.

The faith of the Church rests upon the sufficiency of God, yet the Church has abundantly demonstrated its own insufficiency in interpreting that faith. The Christian revelation has been abused in the house of its friends, both by literalists and by liberals. To begin with, the basic distinction between Biblical and cultural religions has been obscured. Culture religions — and Christianity itself has often lost its supracultural character — seek to achieve the eternal by some discipline of mind or heart, whether mystical or rational. Biblical religion stresses the gulf eternally fixed between the Creator and the creature which neither mysticism nor rationalism can cross; revelation lets down a drawbridge from within the divine, but it is useful only to those who see it. The Christian revelation itself is relativized by every finite mind that accepts it. The worship of a God who is more than man's highest wisdom and virtue makes contrition possible. Every grasp of the revelation is at best an inexact representation, a more or less faithful approximation. This position requires an intellectual humility rare among liberals and literalists alike. Pride has been more common among the interpreters of the faith once for all delivered to the saints. As Helvetius, with much justification, put it: " On every side you see the consecrated knife of religion raised against the breasts of women and children, and the earth all smoking with the blood of victims, immolated to false gods or the Supreme Being, and presenting one sickening, horrible charnel house of intolerance " (*Beyond Tragedy,* pp. 232, 233).

Liberalism, in haste to escape the obscurities of literalism, has often substituted a central relativism for central certainty. In the first place, liberalism has overestimated the role of reason. Revelation is meaningless to purely rational religion, for rationalists always approach life with the naïve confidence that human reason can at length entirely resolve its mystery; rationalists inevitably overlook the embarrassing fact that human reason is always involved in the enigma it seeks to comprehend — indeed is itself the enigma. As Niebuhr sees it, liberalism produces neither warriors nor saints, neither heroes nor rebels, and is always ill at ease when confronted with either their fury or their passion. Presented with a Lenin or a Napoleon on the one hand, or a Francis or a Tolstoy on the other, the gentle liberal can only deplore their fanaticism and regret their ignorance of the principles of sociology. Liberalism has disclosed its effeminacy in its complete lack of asceticism. Some asceticism is a permanent characteristic of all serious religion. It has often degenerated into morbid prudery, but its complete absence is an evidence of the loss of religious vitality. Similarly, there is a millennial hope in every vital religion, and it is usually realistic enough to expect catastrophe. But liberalism has totally surrendered all expectation of judgment; its exclusive evolutionary millennialism is always the hope of the comfortable.

The real weakness of liberalism is its capitulation to the prevailing secularism. There is, in Niebuhr's view, only one step from a reasonable idealism to opportunism, and only another step from opportunism to a dishonest acceptance of the *status quo*. There is no way of measuring the perils of fanaticism against the perils of opportunism, but it is rather obvious that society as a whole is more inclined to inertia than to adventure, and is therefore in greater need of the challenge of the absolutist than the sweet reasonableness of the relativist.

Yet Niebuhr genuinely appreciates the sweet reasonableness of the liberal. From his viewpoint, the contributions of the liberal spirit to social well-being, its tolerance, good will, and rational sympathy, are prematurely discounted in an era like our own because its claims have been too extravagant and its fruits too meager. The liberals are always needed in an established society to minimize racial antagonisms, to preserve harmony between competing groups, to relate specialized functions to one another, and to make tolerable the relations between individuals. In brief, the virtue of the supernaturalists is precisely their vertical dimension; their vice lies in the embarrassing fact that they have no horizontal awareness. Liberalism has lost the virtue of the vertical, but has lost also its horizontal insensitivity. Barnabas is always needed as well as Paul; the feminine is always as necessary as the masculine.

The Church at its best is the repentant community. But repentance, either among literalists or liberals, has seldom been excessive. In classical Christianity it is asserted again and again that repentance is the beginning of redemption, and possibly synonymous with it. On the one hand it makes a difference whether men are good or evil, loving or selfish, honest or dishonest. It makes a real difference, that is, an ultimate difference in the sight of God. On the other hand it makes no difference at all. No life can justify itself ultimately before God. The evil and the good, even the more and the less good, are equally in need of the mercy of the cross. God pays all his servants more than they are worth.

There is, in short, no method by which men can extricate themselves so completely from human conflict that they are worthy to build a temple dedicated to the God from whom we learn " the nothingness of all human victories." There is no way of moral striving to build the Church of God. The Church is created, not by the pride of the Pharisee, but by the humility of the publican; not by the achievement of pure goodness, but by the recognition of human sinfulness. This necessary contrition is the fruit of faith in the transcendent God who cannot be identified with any human goodness.

It is always the task of the prophet to thrust with the sword of criticism. The struggle between the prophets and the pride of Israel contains ultimate insights almost totally lost in modern mediocrity. The prophets sought vainly to prove to Israel that a nation might have a divine mission and yet not be immune to divine judgment. As Niebuhr sees it, the United States, like Israel, must consider both its divine assignment and its human sin.

Today, as much as at any period in history, the prophet's conscience is a social necessity. Modern secularism speaks naïvely about the sociological source of conscience, but the most effective opponents of tyranny today, as always, are persons who can say, " We must obey God rather than men." The prophets' heroism is possible because they have a vantage point from which they can discern the pretensions of the modern Caesars and defy their police states.

The two obvious weaknesses in Niebuhr's system of ideas are also his sources of strength. On the one hand he is wrong in viewing the ethic of Jesus as solely vertical. True, he endlessly asserts that love is an impossible possibility with direct relevance to every social issue, that love may always be achieved, even by sinful men, more perfectly than it is achieved. His negative definition of love as simple heedlessness of self needs more positive content. Love is better understood as responsibility. Responsibility is required of men because responsibility is the nature of God. It was love-as-responsibility that hung upon the cross under the weight of our irresponsible self-love. Nonetheless it is true that love-as-responsibility, rather than as simple selflessness, remains an impossible possibility, always beyond our actual achievement, yet always more perfectly within our reach.

On the other hand no Christian will be quite satisfied with Niebuhr's view that man both has, and has not, divine grace. Every Christian will recognize that sin persists on the highest levels of saintliness, that sin must be forgiven at the end as well as the beginning of the Christian life. The Reformation-Calvin-Luther emphasis has rightly retained this truth when the Arminius-Wesley-sectarian accent has frequently lost it. Nonetheless, you are left on the last page of Niebuhr's fourteen volumes with the feeling that Christ's words, " My grace is sufficient for thee," are not true. This deficiency may be explained by the fact that Niebuhr is always preoccupied with the interior of the Christian's soul, and is insufficiently aware that the Christian gospel has always offered an actual union between Christ and the soul — a marriage, if you like. In this marriage the central interest is not the perpetual, though necessary, agony of sin, repentance, and forgiveness but the perpetual glory of a fellowship that transcends sin. Forgiveness exists for fellowship, not fellowship for forgiveness. A marriage solely preoccupied with sin and forgiveness would be utterly intolerable. Repentance is the basic essential in man, society, and Church, but the purpose is fellowship, and the means forgiveness. In other words, as Niebuhr would himself confess, we are left at the end not only with the insufficiency of man, history, and Church, but also with the insufficiency of Niebuhr. It is Christ after all who must rescue, and restore, our souls.

" The cross is a revelation of the love of God only to those who have first stood under it as a judgment. It is in the cross that the exceeding sinfulness of human sin is revealed. It is in the cross that we become conscious how not only what is worst but what is best in human culture and civilization is involved in man's rebellion against God. It was Roman law, the pride of all pagan civilization, and Hebraic religion, the acme of religious devotion, which crucified the Lord. . . . Our gospel is one which assures salvation in the cross of Christ to those who heartily repent of their sins " (*Ibid.*, pp. 210–211).

THE SUFFICIENCY
OF
GOD

The Postcritical Theology of Nels F. S. Ferré

The Postcritical Theology
of
Nels F. S. Ferré

If Reinhold Niebuhr's theology can be quickly, and essentially, summarized in the word of Jesus, "Without me ye can do nothing," the theology of Nels F. S. Ferré can be similarly summarized in the word of Paul, "I can do all things through Christ which strengtheneth me." The word of Jesus, though expressed negatively, clearly carries Paul's meaning. Put affirmatively, the line would read: "With me ye can do all things." Niebuhr thinks negatively of human sufficiency; Ferré thinks positively of the sufficiency of God. Each theology needs the other: the postcritical faith needs the Niebuhr realism; the critical faith needs Ferré's affirmation of the adequacy of love. Without Ferré, Niebuhr is cynical; without Niebuhr, Ferré is sentimental. Niebuhr has thrust his two-edged sword deep into modern complacence, but where Niebuhr has wounded, Ferré has healed. Niebuhr has turned the modern critical temper upon itself, and has thereby made faith possible but not inevitable. Ferré has built a theology of love upon the ground Niebuhr has cleared. Niebuhr has accented the inadequacy of the human spirit; Ferré has emphasized the adequacy of the Holy Spirit. Where Niebuhr is a John the Baptist, pronouncing doom upon the perennially false, Ferré is a Saint John, announcing the resurrection of the permanently true. It is a caricature to say that Niebuhr sees no possibility of success; it is no caricature to say that Ferré sees no possibility of failure.

A direct look at Ferré's life will disclose that, in his case, theology is a postscript to a divine-human encounter. Paul's experience on the road to Damascus determined the direction, if not the content, of his subsequent thought. Ferré's experience of divine severity and divine goodness laid the foundation of his faith.

Ferré was born in Sweden in 1908, the son of a Baptist minister. He dedicated his first book, *Swedish Contributions to Modern Theology* (1939), to his fire-breathing Fundamentalist father, Rev. Frans Ferré, "for fifty years a minister to Swedish people." Though Nels Ferré eventually departed from literalism, he still retains its depth of seriousness. To him, an easy religion is a false promise; true faith makes radical demands and commands radical treatments. No easy religion was offered him in childhood. Evangelists, more conscious of the horrors of hell than of the glories of heaven, summoned him with fire and brimstone to the mourner's bench, there to confess his sins and be saved. Not to obey the mandate of the Bible was to carry on his forehead the mark of the Beast. Christ was presently to return to judge the world, "perhaps tonight, perhaps tomorrow, but in any case, suddenly and soon." Then the day of opportunity would be ended and the lost would cry in vain for death. A literal hell, with souls bubbling forever in a flaming caldron, produced in Ferré exactly what it produced in Mary Baker Eddy, a firm determination to do away with it.

The Ferré family lived in the country, next to the farm later bought by Greta Garbo. Once when Nels returned to find the family unexpectedly away, his heart turned frigid with fear, the whole world appeared abandoned, and he screamed for the sight of another human. Christ had certainly come, and one raw youth was left alone to face the unspeakable doom. A chilling silence, and hysterical inward shivering, followed. The Fundamentalists seemed more certain of doom than of hope, and the young Ferré was numbed rather than drawn; from the wrath of the Almighty, and from the Almighty, he desired only escape.

But Ferré the elder could preach with joy and confidence about an equally literal heaven. When Nels was twelve, he heard his father speak quietly at a midweek prayer meeting about the future bliss of the saints. Surrounded by friends and neighbors deeply beloved, Nels felt, and has continued to feel, the call of heaven. Deep yearning for the God of Love pressed tears into his eyes, and his mother drew him to his knees. All knelt, and all prayed. Torrents of words gushed forth, and have continued to gush into ten volumes. New converts have seldom prayed so long and so fervently. Jericho's walls had crumbled, and Nels's heart grew light with joy. Late that night his father cautioned him, gently but firmly, that, though saved, he must nevertheless sleep as before. But joy, and a whole new universe, had found him. He was no longer afraid of the dark, and he went at once to share his new-found treasure with a friend.

Ferré confesses that he has been converted three times: the first to traditional Christianity; the second to honesty; and the third to Agape. His own life thus televises the modern Church, wherein he finds three kinds of Christians — the precritical, the critical, and the postcritical. His first conversion was to naïve Fundamentalism, all heart and little head; his second to a thoroughgoing liberalism, what he later terms "the theology of the bootstraps," all head and very little heart; and his third to the Love which is the heart of God and the hope of man.

Ferré's life is a study in tormented spirituality; his second conversion began when "shadows of thought and knowledge crept steadily over the bright expanse of traditional faith." How could Cain and Abel father sons and daughters without female assistance? The elder Ferré drew his son aside and whispered an explanation which was no more and no less than simple incest. How could Noah's ark carry so many animals? Nels's mother urged him not to doubt, but to believe the Bible. Worry pushed into his mind that Christianity, though wonderful, might not be true. "Don't argue with God" was Fundamentalism's only advice and Nels's happiness evaporated like mist before the sun.

At thirteen he came to America to work for his education. In high school he tried to secure peace of soul by social nonconformity; he stayed away from movies, dances, and even Shakespearean plays, but to no avail. Faith was not to be forced, not even by his torrents of words at young people's meetings. High school petting, possibly as present as education is absent, plagued him. He told himself that petting was "natural," yet dared not succumb completely to biology.

Worst of all, and surprisingly enough, not even high school could keep some actual education from creeping through to him. College further presented his naïve faith with rational impossibilities. Came the sciences, history, psychology, Biblical criticism, and a growing feeling that not every picture in the Bible, even of God, was respectably moral. One night he sank down by his bed, a disillusioned junior, and prayed that, if there were any God to hear him, he might be given the courage to be honest. With the collapse of external literalism, God too had disappeared. Once he had defended his punctuation in a high school theme by King James usage, and was certain his teacher was an atheist when she flunked his paper. He felt himself confronted with an ultimate either/or, Christianity or honesty, and he could not but choose honesty. Head and heart went their separate ways, and not until his third conversion could he bring them back together, but minds as well as souls must be born from above. He became, and is still, consciously critical, though he has surrendered both head and heart to Love as the final reality of the world.

Biblicism was gone, but he was further disturbed by a plain contradiction in traditional theology, that the sovereign Lord, proclaimed as saving Love, should finally commit the greater part of mankind to an eternal hell. If it was God's will that all men should be saved, and if with God all things were possible, how could an eternal hell be taken seriously? His maternal grandmother had sometimes muttered meekly about a second chance for those who had had no opportunity in this life to receive Christ. She would do that for her son, she said, and had no doubt that God was better than she. Nels's tender but strong-willed mother had even risked life and limb to present before the family the case of the eternally lost, who had never seen the Light which shone round Galilee. The father then thundered from Mt. Sinai the orthodox damnation, and worlds of thought collided in Nels's mind. As Monica finally won out over Patricius with her son, Augustine, so Nels's mother, in his eventual theology, finally defeated his father. There was no flexibility in the elder Ferré. One condemnation was to be given the hardened, the babes, and the heathen. Man was not to question God. There was no appeal to a higher court, and no postponement of the issue. Family peace, and submission to the father's pontifical utterances, persisted or perished together. But the hidden reservation remained in the child's "unhardened heart and untampered logic of love."

As an Augustus Howe Buck Scholar and Fellow, Nels received his B.A. at Boston University (1931), and entered Andover Newton Theological School. While there, he found the reading of a non-assigned book each week the better part of education. George A. Gordon's *My Education and Religion* provided needed light. Ferré became convinced that it was possible to unite honesty with Christianity, indeed that neither could live without the other. His third conversion had begun, though it was not to be completed without a required graduate course in intense personal suffering. Before reading Gordon, Nels had been held in check by his father's stern view of divine severity. There was suffering in the world, and no place for sentimentality. Gordon convinced him, however, that even in severity, God is Love. God's severity, for Love's sake, as well as his open goodness, has remained central in the Ferré theology. He considers evil a necessary condition of God's control of our freedom. We are neither determined nor irresponsibly free; it is not in our power finally to frustrate the eternal Purpose. We are free to revolt, but within limits, that we may thus learn and accept, in God's long and patient time, his way and his way alone. Through pain and pleasure God leads us to the recognition of our insufficiency, that we may cast our faithlessness upon his faithfulness. Love as kindness, and love as severity, effects God's Purpose in us, if not in this life, then in one or many lives to come.

To perceive this truth with the mind is one thing; to perceive it existentially with the soul is another. In the first conversion Ferré adopted traditional religion, though not without a personal experience of God. In the second conversion, he became free from the imposed past. In the third, conceived by insight, and born of suffering, Ferré found the real God, head and heart agreeing. He was being converted all the while to the same God. Each conversion was an intensification and a redirection of growth. Slowly he has moved from the center in self to the center in God.

He received the B.D. at Andover Newton in 1934, the M.A. (1936) and the Ph.D. (1938) at Harvard. He completed postdoctoral study at the Universities of Uppsala and Lund, and was Sheldon Traveling Fellow from Harvard to Europe. In Sweden he became thoroughly, though not uncritically, indoctrinated in Lundensian theology; he presented this significant material in his first book, *Swedish Contributions to Modern Theology,* where the greater part of his later system of ideas appears in seed form. He accepted Lund's Agape motif, but rejected its nonnormative approach to theology along with its traditional dualism.

He was married in 1932 to Katharine Louise Pond, daughter of Dr. and Mrs. B. W. Pond (M.D.), of Boston. His wife appears, as counselor, typist, and proofreader in all his later books. He dedicated *Faith and Reason* (1946) " to Katharine in love, the bond of perfectness," and *The Christian Faith* (1942) to his wife's father and mother, " parents not only in law, but also in love." Ferré acknowledges that an immeasurable power for conversion came to him through his marriage. An authentic other person entered his world. He possessed a high, zealous theology, wedded to intensity of spirit. His wife's liberal theology centered in constructive and forgiving good will. He pitied her faith; she loved him, through suffering, into newness of life. Just being real came to mean more and more to him. Her quiet, steady faith, her believing prayer, and later, the devoted prayer of family and friends surrounded him with healing grace.

He was ordained a Congregational minister in 1934, and still in his early thirties became professor of theology at Andover Newton. It was then that his salvation through surgery began in earnest. For nine years he was a victim of chronic arthritis. His own description of the ordeal is priceless:

" God was at the center of my theology, yet *I* was at the center of my life — prayer, faith, and work notwithstanding. I was a Harvard doctor of philosophy; I had spent years working on books from five thirty in the morning to eleven or later at night; I had stepped almost at once into a graduate professorship at my own Andover Newton; and I felt too free to correct my colleagues. Exploding with ideas, I talked too much. I wanted to be accepted, but the more I tried to prove myself worthy of belonging, the less welcome I was. . . .

"God knew that I needed to suffer long and hard. Without sentimentality he took away my health and gave me years of pain, of constant physical handicap. Its intensity and duration cannot be known outside the family; in pain dulled by medicine and with an irrepressible drive to be used, I appeared at the line of duty. I dared tell no one how much I was suffering lest I lose my chance of participation. My wife and family are the heroes of those strange years. My wife cared for a baby daughter who was slowly dying during one of my hardest periods. Never can I stop thanking God for the purgatorial fire of those years. In them God's severity became personally accepted as goodness, and part of the process of conversion was actually effected. . . .

"Gradually, . . . God has converted me to patience. He knows what he is doing; he knows long waiting. What right have we to fret, or to try to take the Kingdom by force, even the force of insight? Truth wins slowly, but is never stopped finally. Patience has given me much peace. I was really surprised that with less push came far more acceptance. God's pace, after all, is best for us " (" The Third Conversion Never Fails," in *These Found the Way,* edited by David Wesley Soper, pp. 136, 137. The Westminster Press, 1951).

An essential part of Ferré's suffering was the very intensity of his sense of mission. He felt that he had a commission from God, that his mission and message were certain. In his view, liberalism had relativized and literalism had strait-jacketed Christianity. The shorn Samson, eyeless in Gaza, awaited rescue in the house of bondage. Ferré's task was to proclaim anew that the sovereign Lord is saving Love, that divine Love will not be, and cannot be, denied, that God works through general providence to bring forth the self only in order that special providence may begin in the self the creation of a saint. God is in absolute control; all history and experience are simply the pedagogy of Love. The predictability of nature makes knowledge possible; the precariousness of process makes clear man's insufficiency, in order that he may cast himself utterly on the sufficiency of God. This clue, followed thoroughly, Ferré recognized, would revolutionize modern theology, cut across literalism, naturalism, and liberalism, and exchange new light for old darkness. There is nothing new about the radical (root) idea of God's love, but its final meaning for faith and reason, for the purpose and process of God, for the nature and purpose of evil, and for the Christian view

of last things, was, and remains, to be seen and accepted. To com-
municate his revolutionary idea to fellow Christians everywhere was
Ferré's burning ambition, and his slow acceptance as an authentic
Christian voice increased his cleansing pain. In his words, " All my
life I have had to wait abnormally long for many things which I
wanted in a particular hurry " (*Strengthening the Spiritual Life,*
p. 22. Harper & Brothers, 1951). Yet looking back upon his pilgrimage, the amazing thing is not how slowly, but how quickly, he has
achieved rank among America's leading theologians.

Ten books have come from his busy mind, and it is safe to expect
as many more. Though each presents the same structure of theology,
each is significant in its own way, and, whether heavy or light, of
inestimable value. Ferré has rejected the Lund dualism, and the
Lund descriptive rather than normative theology, yet *Swedish Contributions to Modern Theology,* published in 1939, when Ferré was
thirty-one, accents his heavy indebtedness to Aulén and Nygren on
the depth relation of human Eros to divine Agape. In 1940, when
Ferré was thirty-two, came *The Christian Fellowship,* attacking liberalism as the idolatry of man, and traditionalism as the idolatry of
doctrine, stressing Agape as Christianity's distinctive motif, its principle of inclusiveness and exclusiveness, applicable alike to the Bible
and to all other religious literature; human knowledge and fellowship, which are neither absolute nor valueless, can approach com-
pleteness only through forgiveness and surrender. *The Christian
Faith,* in 1942, relates the push of process to the pull of Purpose,
asserts that Love must work through pain, distinguishes between the
priceless pearl of Love and its inexpensive Biblical setting, denies
that traditionalism's purity of doctrine is an end in itself, pours out
with scorn " the skim milk of liberal theology," finds in the divine
Agape a social gospel without secularism. In 1943 appeared *Return
to Christianity,* a small book with big ideas and probably, along with
Pillars of Faith (1948), the layman's best introduction to Ferré.
Return to Christianity describes and defines the cracked bells of literalism, liberalism, and scientism, with its reductionist anesthetic, diag-
noses the failure of secular education to educate, seeks a more ex-
cellent way than capitalist or socialist materialism, and urges the

acceptance, in theology and in life, of Christianity's full fellowship on earth and in heaven. The Three volumes in series, bearing the continuous subtitle, Reason and the Christian Faith, began with *Faith and Reason,* written in thanksgiving for the return of health, and tracing through science, philosophy, and religion the pointing of process to Purpose. The distinct, and common, tasks of science, philosophy, and theology, and the false uses of all three, have not been better described. The book should be required reading in all college survey courses attempting to make an effective team of these rival prima donnas. Science has not failed man; it is man who has failed science. Philosophy is simply rational knowledge; theology involves the reflexive superspective which looks back upon present process from final Purpose; religion in general is whole response to what is *regarded* as most important and most real; right religion is whole response to what *is* most important and most real. Only by the breaking of self do we change from selves to sons. The series continued with *Evil and the Christian Faith* (1947), wherein Ferré struggles with the problem that has always plagued him in thought and life, but concludes, perhaps prematurely, that evil has only a functional and not at all a final reality. In his view, man may not have two deities, God and pleasure. No vacation-at-the-beach philosophy is adequate for man. The hand of God hurts to heal. The self must rebel in order to be a self, but only that it may become a son. Moral evil is man's misuse of freedom; natural evil is God's control of freedom. All men must, at one time or another, pass through self-sufficiency to self-despair, and thence to God's security in the Agape fellowship. Accepted, dedicated suffering can be placed on God's altar for the redemption of the world. Agape is definitely discontinuous with all religions, became flesh conclusively, but not concludingly, in Jesus Christ for our salvation, can be understood and realized only through the Holy Spirit. *Pillars of Faith,* perhaps the best short summary of essential Christianity, and the best short history of the Christian Church now in print, describes the five authorities upon which the Church has in sequence depended, explains how each has at times become through human sinfulness a problem rather than a power, why all are necessary for the fuller faith —

Jesus, the Holy Spirit, the Church, the Bible, and reasoned experience. Following *Pillars of Faith,* the series "Reason and the Christian Faith" concluded with *Christianity and Society* (1950). The
implications of Agape for man and society are carried out in full.
Christianity is through and through social. Man exists for himself
only that he may live for God and the Fellowship. Nature is both
steady and risky, in order that man may learn responsibility without
self-sufficiency. Creative newness enters the world only through
those whose eyes are open to what is more-than-society. Social theory
needs not only realism, but even more, Reality. When man loses his
heart, his head soon follows. Liberalism spoke in love, but forgot that
it was the truth that was to be spoken. The God of wrath and the
God of love are the same God, working through slow patience and
sudden catastrophe to create and break the self-centered self that it
may become a member of the Family. Man's freedom is finite; he
cannot thwart God eternally. The determinism of Love is final; the
freedom of fear is temporal. Agape is released in individual souls
mostly through prayer. Men cannot pray effectively together who do
not pray rightly alone. The business of theology is to look at life
from the perspective of the Ultimate. The year 1951 brought to print
two penetrating volumes, one food for the people, the other giraffe's
food. The first, meager in size but not in insight, is *Strengthening
the Spiritual Life,* a Christian muezzin, a call to prayer, a command
to worship, to work, and hardest of all to wait, in the Holy Spirit.
The second, meager neither in weight nor in light, builds a long-
needed bridge across the chasm from Kierkegaard to Aquinas, *The
Christian Understanding of God.* The importance of this book, the
first of what may prove ten volumes in series on Christianity's central ideas, corrected by Agape, cannot be overestimated. All of Ferré
is in this volume, though the full portrait may be more apparent to
one who has taken the grand tour through his earlier writing. Basically, the idea is that theology, like philosophy, has always been
falsely centered either in being or becoming, in Reality conceived
as static perfection, or in Reality conceived as dynamic process. In
Ferré's view Agape terminates this historic controversy and makes
of the two hemispheres one world. Being must endlessly become in

order to be what it is. Love is ultimate, and never less than itself, but freely and endlessly creates to share its joy, and as it creates it grows. Over against the infinity of being is the infinity of nonbeing, of nothingness, but nothingness constitutes no barrier to God. Every divine creation, every self, and every self broken and embraced by the Holy Spirit, enriches and enlarges Love. The Spirit of God has driven the evolutionary process from below, impersonally, to bring forth the self-conscious self, the natural man, predominantly possessed by Eros, in order that the self, at the end of itself, may be possessed directly by Agape, the Holy Spirit; it is he who makes of isolated selves the Community of saints, the Fellowship for which the world was made and is now sustained. *Process,* yes; *Reality,* yes; but Process *and* Reality, and the Process in the service of Reality. Reality is the divine Agape conclusively but not concludingly enacted in the whole Christ, neither Jesus alone nor the Church alone, but Head and body together. A basic limitation, traceable in the total Ferré theology, is the category of Antibeing, noticeable by its absence. In Ferré's view, nothing can, nothing does, permanently resist Agape. Love never fails. Resistance is only the pedagogically necessary self-centeredness of man on the way from his center in self to his center in God. Hell has a school and a door in it, and no man can finally be lost. The volume, and the whole Ferré theology, fails to take into account the obvious evolutionary fact that not all that starts finishes, that not every amoeba becomes a monkey, that not every monkey becomes a man, that not every man becomes a saint; on Jesus' terms, few do. Thank God that papa crocodile eats ninety-five out of every hundred eggs mama crocodile lays. That which is born of the flesh is flesh; only that which is born of the Spirit has resurrection in its future. Nonetheless, in itself, Ferré's view of the nature and purpose of God is final; no work will be found more ultimately satisfying, nor more ultimately true, for the Christian, or for any man. God is Agape, and Agape precisely unites being and becoming, Reality and Process. In his first work Ferré was content to leave the future of the natural man in God's hands, tentatively accepting the Lundensian idea that the problem is beyond the limits of faith. From that time on, Ferré has not been content to leave the problem in God's hands, but has closed his system on the note of inevitable universal salvation. In his own words, a closed system is closed seeing; theology always suffers at the hands of the scheme makers. In Ferré's faith, Calvin's determinism of Power has been subtly changed into a determinism of Love. To him, Love is ultimately irresistible. Yet is it not the very nature of Love to be resistible? In Ferré's own words, Love invites, and never forces. Perhaps Love is ultimately irresistible to those who are born of Love, but to those who remain centered in self Love is precisely an unreality, an illusion; it is not seen ultimately; it is therefore neither perceived, accepted, nor rejected. Ferré believes every theologian is finally forced to choose either universal salvation or a limited God; but when an unlimited God selects a process, among alternate possibilities, he is obviously limited by the process he selects; hence, Ferré has presented a false either/or. In any case, every Christian will recognize, with Ferré, that it is not Love that fails but self-love.

For many years professor of theology at Andover Newton Theological School, Nels F. S. Ferré became in February, 1950, professor of philosophical theology at the Vanderbilt University School of Religion. When he gave the Cole Lectures at Vanderbilt, he was asked to name the conditions on which he might accept a Vanderbilt invitation. His conditions, among them to give one lecture a day five days a week that he might be released for further writing, were accepted, and the change was made. In 1952, Ferré lectured at Mansfield College, Oxford, on leave of absence from Vanderbilt.

He is endlessly in demand at ministers' conferences and summer schools; colleges continually seek him for religious emphasis weeks. In the spring of 1951, Beloit students were stirred as never before to deep questioning, of themselves and of their total universe. Ferré does the work of two, possibly three, men. If only there were more of him! His presence searches the heart, stretches the mind, and blesses the spirit. He preaches, and practices, love. Daily he lifts his friends, and his enemies, near and far, and by name, to God in prayer, and follows each prayer with a personal card or letter full of insight, counsel, and encouragement. This writer must confess from experience that a Ferré note out of the blue sets the soul singing.

He has given the Wells Lectures at Texas Christian University, the Gay Lectures at Southern Baptist Theological Seminary, the Hyde Lectures at Andover Newton Theological School, the Denio Lectures at Bangor Theological Seminary, the Earl Lectures at the Pacific School of Religion, the Cole Lectures at Vanderbilt, the Rall Lectures at Garrett Biblical Institute, and the Hoff Lectures at Bethany Biblical Seminary. He is an active member of many national committees devoted to philosophy, theology, social studies, and higher education. His influence, already great, is growing, and will grow. He is probably the only theologian now living who is continuously invited as a lecturer by both Unitarians and Nazarenes. He precisely unites liberalism and literalism, and transcends both. He lives fully in both vertical and horizontal dimensions. In his words:

"Gratitude to God and to . . . near ones in the Spirit increases my desire to become thoroughly converted, consciously and subconsciously. Without reserve I have put my life on God's altar to be used for the common good; ever more I want to trust his faithfulness to take complete charge of my life.

"The first time I was converted, in content, to traditional Christianity; the second time, to honesty; the third time, to the love of God and men, first in theology and gradually in life. Beyond the third conversion, however, there can be no step ahead except of the same kind. The third conversion was to the love of God, in thought and in life; in the end that cannot fail, for firm is the promise, 'Love never fails,' for love is of God and is God" ("The Third Conversion Never Fails," in *These Found the Way,* p. 138).

GOD IS LOVE

To Ferré, theology and life are one. Yet it is important, and necessary, to examine in detail his system of ideas.

To begin with, it may be well to examine Ferré's assertion that scientism, traditionalism, and liberalism have all failed, both theoretically and practically, to understand either God or the world. This is a large statement, but the truth is larger than the statement. In Ferré's words:

"Science as a self-sufficient way to truth failed theoretically because by the limitations inherent in its own method it tells us nothing final about the nature of ultimate truth; it failed practically because its new informa-

tion and physical achievements must always be subject to a moral drive
and direction which it could not provide. . . . Traditional theology failed
theoretically because it was not consistent with Christianity's central
affirmation that God is all-powerful and all-wise love, and because it reduced God's absolute scale of magnitude to its own infinitesimal drop of
historic time. Traditional theology also failed practically because it became
generally allied with the *status quo* in the world of politics, economics,
and social customs, and was not a daring prophetic power for the transformation of all the relationships of men.

"Modernism failed theoretically because it gave up the Christian faith
itself as the primary standard of truth, accepting instead as primary the
secondary standards of reason and experience in so far as these could
demonstrate the truth of religion in terms of what is here and now actual; it failed practically as well because its inner intellectual inconsistency choked off its religious drive. Faith is power. The Christian faith,
when central in thought and practice, can heal and transform all of life.
This power modernism lacked. Thus while traditional theology was not
Christian enough, modernism was not religious enough. Now, freed from
the false claims of science, we must accept resolutely in thought and life
the Christian faith which is God's power of salvation for both the individual and society. . . .

"The primary Christian claim is not theoretical but practical. It is that
there *is* a power not our own that can lift and lead us into the reality of
fellowship. . . . There are those who have showed us the power of
Christian love when men surrender themselves fully to it. . . . Christianity definitely does not offer to solve this problem theoretically alone,
and stresses, therefore, that little has been done until the hearts of men
as well as all their social patterns are increasingly subject to the claim of
God's Agape. This is the *locus of solution* of man's problems. To depart
from it is to fail; to walk in it is to find real victory" (*Return to Christianity*, pp. 13, 14, 23, 24. Harper & Brothers, 1943).

Modern education has similarly failed, and it has failed primarily
to educate. Its failure is due to a false philosophy of history and human nature; the depths and stubbornness of evil have not been
sufficiently acknowledged; its sophisticated negativism has produced
critical and clever but seldom appreciative and creative minds; and
its analytical method has sacrificed man's peculiar heritage, his creative and spiritual capacities, on the altar of quantitative measure-
ments and sense proofs.

Where Niebuhr's method is criticism, turning negativism upon itself, Ferré's method is primarily affirmation. He begins and ends with Christianity as beyond equation with any form of human culture; while it is continuous with man, its significance lies precisely in the fact that it is always discontinuous with him as well. To Ferré the abiding truth of conservative theology stands: Christianity is ultimate; it is unique and absolute. He is certain that we cannot reduce the oceanic mysteries of God to the tin cup of human reason. Prior to God's supreme Revelation, primarily not a station-to-station but a person-to-person disclosure, we simply did not know what God most deeply is and wants; but now through the Agape-made-flesh, though we know only partly, we nevertheless know truly. We cannot know God absolutely, yet in Jesus Christ we know the absolute. The very center of Christianity is God's special, final Revelation and his special, conclusive redemption in Jesus Christ. The Virgin birth, which every Christian experiences in the birth of the Spirit, and regardless of the biological issue, stands for the real fact of a special discontinuity entering the continuity of history. Christianity, precisely defined, is a God-centered, God-given freedom and faithfulness in fellowship based on the kind of love first fully revealed and made effective as light and life in Jesus Christ. Self-giving love creative of fellowship is the human ultimate. But this is also Christianity. Christianity, therefore, is at least good humanism.

It is one thing to say this; it is another to apply it throughout the length and breadth of religion. Ferré is quick to point out that Christianity has, in itself, both a principle of inclusion and a principle of exclusion. The one, proceeding from the nature of Agape, precludes Christianity's invidious comparison with other religions, and at the same time requires that we learn whatever is good in other religions. The other cleanses historic Christianity of its subagapaic idolatries — its alternate worship of the Church, the Bible, or reason and experience; in the same movement it cleanses the subgood from the good in all other religions. The principle of inclusion is this: all things cultural, intellectual, moral, and spiritual which are consistent with the God-centered, sacrificial, creative good will first fully revealed and made effective in Jesus Christ may be freely admitted into the Christian religion. The principle of exclusion is like unto it: all that is inconsistent in profession and practice with the nature of Christianity as sacrificial, creative good will, centered in God and first fully revealed and made effective in Jesus Christ, must be done away. If the Christian Church has been right in keeping the Old Testament with its predominantly sub-Christian content, why cannot Christianity do the same with the Confucian or Hindu scriptures? All religious literature, and indeed all literature of any kind, interpreted in the light of Agape, is permanently available to the growing Christian. Similarly, Ferré finds that the New Testament itself does not always square with its own highest standard, Agape. He thus, perhaps prematurely, side-steps Jesus' recurring words about the broad road to destruction and the narrow road to life, about the many who are called and the few who are chosen. To Ferré, Jesus' words about the salvation of the few are existentially but not ultimately true; they are true of process, but not of Purpose, not of final achievement. He acknowledges, as a present but not a final fact, that few and far between are the saints so buried with God in Christ that their lives are constantly transfigured by the Holy Spirit.

Ferré is at pains to assert, again and again in his books, that he is not aware of any non-Christian literature where the full idea of God's Agape appears. Stoicism emphasized love, but stoic love was impersonal, pantheistic, immanentistic, and self-seeking; it was in no sense a disclosure of the nature of God. The highest insight in Buddhism was not in the teachings of Buddha, which were negative, bent upon the destruction of evil desire, but in his life, in his return from vision to help his fellow men; again, no statement is evident about Love as the nature of God. The Hindu bhakti sects, in their emphasis upon devotion, owe something to Christianity, which predates them, yet essentially accent not Agape but an emotional Eros. The Chinese *jen* stresses mutual benevolence; it is therefore ethical and calculating, and not at all a statement about the nature of God. Lao-tse urged that injury be recompensed with *Teh,* not kindness; there is no disclosure of the full Agape. Confucius expressly prohibited kindness to the evil; his whole system was centered in human morality, not in divine Love. The fifty-third chapter of Isaiah, perhaps the purest expression of vicarious suffering in the Old Testament, is essentially an insight into Israel's historical purpose, not a disclosure of the nature of God. Hosea 11:9 declares, "I will not destroy; I am God and not man." Hosea's love reached out to heal the fallen, and is thus similar to the Christian Agape, but since he recognized no personal need of repentance, his contribution is ambiguous. Isaiah 1:18 approaches the Christian Agape: "Though your sins be as scarlet, they shall be as white as snow"; in the original the second line may have been a question: "Shall they be as white as snow?" The context, which argues for a negative answer, accents unremitting judgment; God's wrath is primary, his love secondary; divine wrath is something other than an expression of divine love. Psalm 103:13 declares that God is a Father who pities his children; it is thus similar to the Christian Agape, but it is only "them that fear him" whom he pities. Apocryphal literature accents law or wisdom as central in God; it emphasizes love as conduct, not as the nature of the Ultimate. Plato's Shepherd of Mankind, in the context, stresses divine reasonableness, not divine self-giving. Ferré concludes:

"Outside Christianity, although there are certain ideas similar to that of the Christian idea of Love, the resemblances are largely superficial. We can say with some confidence that Agape is not only the determinative but also the distinctive motif of the Christian religion, the deepest truth in the universe and the highest ethical standard for man" (*The Christian Fellowship*, p. 87. Harper & Brothers, 1940).

Ferré's view of the nature of God successfully bridges the chasm from Roman architecturalism to Protestant personalism, from Aquinas and Aristotle to Kierkegaard, from the hierarchy of science, philosophy, and theology to pedagogical process, from a motionless to a moving deity, from static perfection to dynamic evolution. God is Love, and Love always remains itself, and is thus motionless in character; at the same time it is always active, dynamic, dramatically creating, directing, and redeeming, in order to be what it is. Love is thus the energy, and the goal, of all evolution. It is above and beyond process, yet perpetually at work within it. God's impersonal energy, the Spirit of God, has driven, and now drives, the total evolutionary process from below to bring forth the self-conscious self, the Eros man. Until each man is in truth an individual, fellowship either divine or human is impossible. Each man in some measure must rebel against divine and human authority to be in reality a self. Original sin is therefore an original necessity, but only for a pedagogical purpose. The self must choose itself in order to be a self, but this only that it may eventually yield itself to God. The purpose may be, and is, frustrated, and thus arises man's misuse of good, his sinfulness, his complacent self-centeredness. God's Agape created Eros to make persons real, to prevent absorption. Eros must precede Agape as man's dominant drive, in order that a fellowship of real persons might be created. This is Ferré's view of the problem of evil, of what is called the Fall. He arrives therefore, as he begins, with an ultimate *monism.* God as Love constitutes the nature of ultimate being. This monism intrinsically involves a dynamic *dualism,* because nonbeing, a help and not a hindrance to monism, serves functionally the purposes of dualism. This monism also includes derivative, yet distinct *pluralism,* wherein man, time, and nature are real, according to their own nature. God is the primary order of reality; man is the secondary; and nature is the tertiary. The only thing missing in this formula is the category of antibeing. As Edwin Lewis has seen, something in the universe resists God's love. Man himself can become the incarnation of this resistance. Aggressive wars are real; the cross of Christ is real; human destruction, of soul as well as of body, is real. Ferré's partial pacifism, which acknowledges the necessity of policemen, which even acknowledges the occasional necessity of the dirty work of war; Ferré's idea of universal salvation, here or hereafter; indeed Ferré's democratic socialism: all issue from the total absence of the category of antibeing in his structure of thought. To him, antibeing is not ultimate but historical; it is an ultimate illusion rising from man's existential and sinful self-love; evil exists in the divine pedagogy only to bring all men through Eros to despair, and thence to Agape. Evil is real existentially, historically, actually, but not ultimately. God on the cross suffers only in history, not in heaven; the cross is the means to human redemption, a sacrifice to a temporal not an eternal evil. No final antibeing exists, or can exist, to thwart the divine Purpose, made flesh in Jesus Christ. What is in itself inconsistent with divine Agape is consistent with divine pedagogy. No Christian can deny that Ferré is right about the divine Purpose, else Agape is not Agape. Yet science at this point may offer revelation to theology; not all raw material becomes a finished masterpiece; not all that starts finishes. Neither creation nor redemption is so simple as that. Without the shedding of blood there is no remission, no creation, no redemption, no fellowship. That which is not fellowship cannot be, and will not be, admitted into fellowship. Only " the pure in heart " shall see God. It is the very nature of Love to invite, not coerce; it is therefore ultimately resistible, particularly to those whose self-love makes them the blind who lead or the blind who follow. Ferré's view, in Baptist theology, is true of the redeemed: once in grace, always in grace. On Ferré's terms, all men are in general grace and on their way to special grace. As he sees it, neither the redeemed nor the unredeemed can ever be lost, only completed in a completion that is never complete, through a dozen purgatories or ten heavens, for not even in eternity can man exhaust the knowledge or the love of God. Ferré simply erases the distinction between the redeemed and the unredeemed; the distinction has only a pedagogical or existential, not an ultimate, validity. Nonetheless, every Christian will agree with Ferré that all men exist for one purpose, to be born again from Eros to Agape by the Holy Spirit. The Spirit of God, the Agent of creation, brings forth the self, only in order that the Holy Spirit, the Agent of redemption, may make of the self the saint. God's impersonal or passive presence is nowhere absent from creation; it is everywhere present in one way or another, in the evolutionary process, in natural man, in the State. God's personal or active presence in history is in the Holy Spirit through the Church. Only in the Holy Spirit can man know God or Christ; only in the Holy Spirit can man love his brother; only in the Holy Spirit does the Church exist. General providence is God's indirect presence in the total process; special providence is his selective and personal control of the total process for the sake of the elect. Men without the Holy Spirit live only, or mainly, under general providence; men in the Holy Spirit live totally in principle, and increasingly in practice, under the selective and personal care of special providence.

Agape as the nature of God is absolute; the absolute Word came conclusively in Jesus; no *other* absolute therefore can possibly come. Yet the same absolute may come repeatedly; the more Christ is repeated in the saint and in the Church, the more he reveals, and realizes, his reality.

So important to Ferré is inevitable universal salvation that he can never let it alone. In his view, an eternal hell is naturally out of the question, both as subjustice — for finite man cannot sin infinitely — and as sublove. To him, hell is the reduction of evil to order by its separation from the good and its control on its own terms. Hell is precisely an instrument of justice in the service of reclamatory Love. Hell is not heaven unattained, but heaven temporarily rejected. Hell cannot be eternal, but it can be longer than we think. Hell is for the unrepentant, purgatory for the repentant. Heaven cannot be heaven until it has emptied hell. In the Ferré rigorism, no saint can enter heaven until all sinners are redeemed. To say the least, this postpones things a bit. Man has the freedom to be over against God, but has no freedom to remain an eternal problem child. Yet, Ferré insists, fear must be preached, for unless we repent we shall all likewise perish. This is the eternal truth of God and of his Word for us. But the severity of God will lead us along with his goodness to our eventual repentance. Our process must end in God's way with a heaven which is the consummation of the Beloved Community, God's own Family.

Ferré is positive about universal salvation, yet with rare humility leaves a door open to possible fuller truth. As he puts it, think we must, but never confuse our thinking with God's.

SOCIETY IS THE SCHOOL OF FELLOWSHIP

In Ferré's view, it is the business of the theologian, not alone to examine all things from the perspective of the ultimate, but also to relate organically the eternally ultimate to the immediately practical. It goes without saying that history is subject to endless improvement; at the same time, one must understand that society cannot be changed by its own power. The more-than-society is the hope of society. God rather than history is central in Christian social thinking. We cannot be saved as society without the mystery of the *more* than society, the ground of our being and thinking. Though we must remember humbly that even in revelation, it is *man,* and not God, who does the seeing, we cannot but recognize that all hope of progress lies in the eternal Purpose beyond all historic process.

The significance of history is precisely freedom. Every human choice is related, positively or negatively, to Agape; our choices are genuinely real in relation to the absolute, yet they are not absolute choices; only God can choose absolutely. Moral evil is our misuse of freedom; natural evil is God's control of our freedom. Evil is actually, but not metaphysically, real. Evil is divine pedagogy within historic process; it has no existence in eternal being. The purpose, and failure, of history is to realize a God-centered freedom-in-fellowship. Since infallibility belongs only to God, no historical authority should regard itself as absolute; to accept any human authority as final is idolatry; it is surrender to the demon of the *status quo.* Socrates, the saints, and the Saviour were, and are perennially, sacrificed to the Molech of human absolutism. We need to know the presence of Purpose now, but also to see that it has as yet been realized only in anticipation. In Jesus Christ and his Church the Anticipation was made flesh.

The basic historical problem is the relation between society and the self. We shall progress farther in social thinking when we understand that *before history* man is neither hopelessly good nor hopelessly bad. *Before God* man in repentance recognizes himself to be totally forgiven and totally unforgivable, but not *before man.* Those who declare man radically bad know the stubbornness of man's sin but not its pedagogical purpose. Sin is the perversion of Eros by finite freedom. Eros is necessary for all finite creatures, and not in itself evil, for God has made it. God has given us Eros to prevent absorption, to make us real and free. Those who declare man radically good see the purpose of the self but not its perversion. The conflict between self and society, whether more or less acute, exists in the saint as well as in the sinner. No human has been completely concerned about and none has been completely indifferent to social good. There is no self that is not in part a socius; there is no socius that is not in part a self.

The problem is complicated by the fact that every man must learn to accept and to love himself genuinely. Self-love is wrong only when it makes the self an ersatz deity. True self-love is the death of the aristocratic self and the self's rebirth within the Agape fellowship. None can accept himself, or find himself acceptable, until he has learned to hate his partial, narrow, defensive self — the self that seeks itself and denies its neighbor and God. Total evil, on Ferré's terms, is impossible for any creature. Man is perverted, partially depraved, or, in truer perspective, an immature child, dominantly selfish, yet deep down bored with his self-seeking and yearning for fellowship.

The Christian faith is totally world-transcending, yet its world-transcendence is totally *for* society. Man's task is to *learn* that God's will is social, that society is the direct object of God the Verb as well as God the Noun. Yet God's love is short-circuited, and his fellowship frustrated, when society wears either a Roman or a Russian strait jacket.

Christianity's world-renunciation, which is also totally *for* society, is precisely the world's conscience. For society's sake a Christian may refuse to participate in war; for the same reason a Christian may accept his share in war's dirty discipline, rejecting the irresponsibility of the pious. When the world steers off the course, whether in imperialistic war or in isolation from the common effort to resist it, the Christian must stay on the course, not to withdraw from the world for the sake of the course, but to keep the course for the sake of the world. As Woodrow Wilson put it, " I would rather fail in a cause I know must someday triumph, than win in a cause I know must someday fail." A Kentucky mountaineer expressed it more simply: " I would rather chase a rabbit and not catch it, than chase a skunk and catch it."

The purpose of society, to the Christian, is not justice but fellowship. Every religion of justice is sub-Christian; it is built on law and invidious comparison. Christianity is a religion of complete concern for all. The Bible contains both the light of true Agape and the darkness of subagapaic justice. The Bible, designed as a royal help, is sometimes a royal hindrance. Much of the Bible's explicit ethics requires a humble and resigned acceptance of the *status quo,* as in Paul's Epistle to Philemon. The higher Biblical ethic can be only the full implication and application of Agape, the Word become flesh for the salvation of self and society.

In Ferré's view, while the Church is created, directed, and disciplined by the Holy Spirit, the State is created, directed, and disciplined by the Spirit of God. The State exists of, by, and for the natural man, and for the saint-in-process who remains, in greater part, natural rather than spiritual. The Spirit of God is God's activity on all levels below Agape, whether in instruction, judgment, or forgiveness. The Holy Spirit is God's activity on the level of Agape. The distinction is functional, not metaphysical. God is not undifferentiated being. The Spirit of God is the pedagogical face and hands of the Holy Spirit. The God of wrath and the God of love are one, but God assumes, in the State, the shape of the avenger to the disobedient. General social action is the field of the Spirit of God, Christian social action the field of the Holy Spirit. Neither the separatist-quietist nor the social gospel was genuinely Christian. The modern approach to social need has been largely physical or spatial, rather than spiritual. Social effort has been primarily externalistic and legislative, the forcing of the good, the compelling of the Kingdom of God. Pietist effort, on the other hand, has been solely internal, accenting conversion and regeneration within the circle of the elect, wholly unaware that Reality unites the inside and the outside without confusing them. The sword of the Spirit is two-edged.

Simple pacifism overlooks God the Creator in its preoccupation with God the Redeemer. If man is determined to use only uncontaminated means, he must needs go out of the world. Absolute pacifists confine Christianity to the level of redemption, as though God were not the Creator, and as though they were too good to do the dirty work that God has to do for our sake, through the austere and unsentimental operation of his wrath, a vital function, it must be remembered, of the Spirit of God. The surrendered Christian must use the best available means to accomplish the best relevant ends. The use of the best available means is not compromise, but obedience to God's actual will. Jesus did not sin by paying tribute money to a corrupt State. History knows little of perfect means. Jesus had to live one way with the world and another way with his disciples. Indeed, the secular world with its understanding of practical issues is often the conscience of the Church, even as the Church in its distinctive realm is the conscience of the world.

When a higher conception comes in, the old gods exist as idols, either openly or in disguise. The Old Testament God has become in large part an idol. Natural conflict, under the Spirit of God, is often preferred to genuine Agape under the Holy Spirit. Man is warlike in nature, warless in grace. Ferré expects the world to move perhaps too quickly from nature to Agape, though he is fully aware that it is a long way from man's animal history to his Agape history. Ferré is realistic enough to see the present as God's way. God has made this kind of world for our salvation; we have therefore no right to deny that wars, however indirectly, have a pedagogical place in it. Yet Ferré is idealistic enough to see that the present exists not for itself, but for the future. In his words:

" Animals and men fight for food to eat, shelter, for their own needs, and then for place and prestige among themselves. But part of this need, curiously and significantly enough, seems to be the need to fight. They need to become themselves through fighting. Fighting seems to be a creative need, beyond mere self-preservation. In one stage of our lives, at least, God has made us to fight. Strife exists in order to differentiate individuals and groups for the sake of preparing them for fuller and better community. Group conflicts and war are, thus, part and parcel of growing men and growing history. The fighting game brings out the whole man in an active challenge. Many have found themselves in war; many have there awakened a sleeping heroism, a sense of importance, a sense of responsibility and concern, who are bored insufferably in peacetime, dabbling away at impersonal tasks that lack challenge. Even the Christian faith must be the Christian conflict. Unless Christianity has within its very bosom the drive to conflict and to war, it has not the full solution to our concrete problems " (*Christianity and Society*, pp. 189–191. Harper & Brothers, 1950).

On Ferré's terms, the Christian can and must renounce war, without renouncing the constructive force of civil government under judicial process, and without renouncing the constructive role of world police. Absolute pacifism is based on a faulty theology which refuses to accept the share of process in God's Purpose. Agape is never a compromise because it uses imperfect means; history, itself an imperfect means, exists to be perfected. Force in itself is no compromise. God uses force continually and is not compromised. God uses physical compulsion and his children must do so too, or evade their responsibility on the level of creation. God takes life. Agape always chooses the most constructive historical alternative, redemptively and creatively. To declare that the use of imperfect means is *ipso facto* compromise is to deny process as the method of God's Purpose, to claim, in fact, to be better than God. Yet when common measures for justice are considered sufficient, then indeed has the Christian lost his savor and become no better than the world. "These [things] ye ought to have done, and not to have left the other undone." Wars between nations, in Ferré's view, belonged (more properly *belong*) to the historic epoch, when the nation served a necessary purpose in God's pedagogy as an expression of natural law. Perhaps prematurely, Ferré believes that this epoch is now past or passing, and with it the place of the State as a sovereign entity under God. As he sees it, the State has a right to demand obedience only as long as it serves a real purpose under God and uses legitimately the power which divine Love has bestowed upon it. When its purpose is past, or when it uses its delegated power illegitimately, as in an unjust war, or in a generally nonconstructive war, the citizen must refuse to obey, serving God rather than men, or even serving his reason and conscience rather than the reason and conscience of men blinded by narrow vision and narrower loyalty. If a Christian, or any other person, is convinced that more can be conserved or created by common action against aggression than without it, he must follow his conscience in this regard, and no one is to judge his decision. Obviously, there is little hope for world fellowship except through the surrender of force to an inclusive and responsible authority; force without a common spirit and mind will never give us a peaceful world.

Attention must be given to Ferré's significant treatment of economics as applied theology. All property is from God, and exists for freedom and fellowship. Individual man needs property both to internalize and externalize himself. Yet power welding rather than frustrating fellowship is the purpose of property in the divine economy. Power can be socialized because it is God's gift for society. Property is both *from* God and *for* men. Property is precisely a means of freedom and faithfulness in fellowship. In one sense, property is freedom from God, freedom over against God. For our own good, God has made us considerably independent of himself. Property bestows on man a necessary pedagogical freedom. Individual initiative and personal enterprise are essential, and any system that denies the individual these necessities goes against the grain of God's purpose with property. Man also needs freedom from things by having enough of them. Reasonable material security is a basic essential. Poverty, which is lack of life, is not God's will for man; poverty is the occasion of envy in the poor as property is the occasion of pride in the rich. Yet the other half of the coin must also be seen. Psychopathic defenders of capitalism will tolerate no restriction upon individual initiative or personal enterprise. They are liberal only in their wish to be liberated from social responsibility. No man can hold private property as a divine right to the detriment of public good. When an individual has what society needs and can profitably use, it is no longer his.

Granted an imperfect and sinful soul, power tempts to pride, to self-importance, to hardness of heart, to imperialistic desire, to irresponsible self-indulgence. Hand in hand with spiritual rebirth must come the socialization of the means of production. Capitalism has enriched our lives and preserved the freedom without which we become submen, yet it is essentially the materialism of the classes, as Communism is the materialism of the masses. Marx without question voiced the envy of the underloved, yet he was also a prophetic personality who expressed the revolt of conscience against the unconcern and iniquity of industrial society. Marxism is bad theology and bad anthropology, and consequently bad sociology and economics. Nevertheless it is not unthinkable that Marxism may be the scourge of God and at the same time God's means to Christian fulfillment. Whatever degree of Christian socialism may be achieved, it must never lose its democratic structure. Without democratic process public ownership is inevitably totalitarian. Creative freedom must always be defended, perhaps through blood, sweat, and tears, against frustrating bureaucracy. State control or ownership, without democratic process, ends in the paralysis of bureaucracy, political oppression, the deadening of creative drive, indifference, officiousness, pride of place and power, irresponsibility, and " passing the buck." Yet these evils are present in any and all systems, for they are part of our actual human nature. Nothing historical is manproof. The primary battle is always spiritual. No change in externals, however drastic, will usher in the Kingdom.

Every sensitive conscience will feel the sting of Ferré's words:

" For Christianity property is never static but always functional. Economic resources are the God-given means and media of fellowship. They are not first of all private possessions, but rather responsibilities entrusted by God for the sake of the common welfare. Property belongs, first of all, to God, has been given by him for social purposes, and no individual or group is ever more than a steward of it. Property belongs to the self as a socius, for property is primarily social in origin, function, and meaning. Profiteering is in essence anti-Christian. What is euphemistically called ' free enterprise ' actually means freedom mostly for the strong — those who possess the means of production or have the skill to attain such control. There is no parallel freedom for the masses of men, but rather an oppressive preconditioning to economic, social, and cultural poverty and dependence because of this very antisocial freedom of the strong " (*Return to Christianity*, pp. 64, 65).

The Church Is Fellowship

Not the least of Ferré's contributions is the tremendous impetus he gives to new vitality in the Church. To him simply and truly the Church *is* the Mission. The Church is God's will for men; it is the fellowship of, by, and in the Holy Spirit. However far below Agape the actual churches may be, and undoubtedly are, they exist only to bring forth saints-in-fellowship, the true Church. If nature and history are God's activity in creation, the Church is his activity in redemption. The specific function of the Church is redemptive; that is its purpose for being; the Church must be in but not of the world; when the Church conforms to secular society and temporal power, it becomes a light set under a bushel. The Church is God's redemptive agency in history demanding for the sake of the world that the creative order conform increasingly to the redemptive goal. The Church *is,* and the churches must become, the pull of God's Purpose in history, the transforming discontinuity through which alone the continuity of process can be redeemed.

Christianity is not a philosophy. Christianity is a fellowship which creates philosophy. The Christian philosophy is the interpretation of history in the light of God's Revelation in Jesus Christ. The purpose alike of creation and redemption is consistent with the truth of God's self-disclosure in Christ; it cannot be less than increasing fellowship through Christ. The Church begins when the human heart, in self-despair, is surrendered to the Holy Spirit, but the Church began historically with the Love of God made flesh at Bethlehem and Pentecost. In Jesus, God's Agape visited man in matchless fullness. Agape pre-existed from all eternity, was in the beginning with God, and was God, "and without him was not any thing made that was made." Not God as Father, but God as Son, was in Jesus. Not the totality of God's being, but the quality of God's nature, became man. The human process of the Bible in no way lessens its disclosure of divine Purpose. Jesus Christ in the Bible is a precious Gift wrapped in inexpensive paper. Some see the Gift in the wrapping but cannot distinguish between them. Others are offended by the wrapping and throw the Gift away. In Ferré's view, if the issue were forced, we should rather keep the wrapping with the Gift than lose the Gift. There is, as he sees it, more danger in superficial liberalism than in undiscriminating fundamentalism. We must always distinguish between the sophisticated skepticism of men " wise in their own conceits," and the true criticism of men who can criticize their own criticism and acknowledge their own ignorance.

In Niebuhr's view, the human problem is insoluble with human resources. Ferré agrees, but insists that the human problem is equally insoluble without human resources. In our day when man-centered moralism goes one way and an irrational God-centeredness the other, we, like Augustine, must realize that no theory of the atonement, or of the Church, can be adequate without sufficient stress on Jesus as our Example, for this alone makes fellowship possible, or without adequate insistence that salvation is of God, since without him we are utterly helpless. Without God we cannot be saved, but neither can we be saved unless we accept the process.

The Church is precisely the fellowship of the Holy Spirit — God's movement through and beyond history. In Ferré's words:

" Christ's death released a redemptive force in history which is peculiarly perpetuated by God's Holy Spirit through the redemptive fellowship which is the Church — a fellowship of grace, a fellowship of forgiveness, wherein by worship and by trust in a personal Saviour man is able to alter his ways and even to become a channel of God's grace into history. No one can *live* orthodox Christianity without creating around him a Christian fellowship. Christianity is the redemptive spirit of Christ flowing through history. . . There can be no experience more final for man than to face the Christ, to surrender to him, and to live eternally within the Christian fellowship of forgiveness, completely dependent upon the grace of God " (*The Christian Faith,* pp. 166, 167, 181. Harper & Brothers, 1942).

For the Church, there are important truths in neglected doctrines, among them the doctrine of the ascension of Christ. He had to be lifted up above all earthly things, for in him was, and is, the eternal reality of God. Only as we see Christ above the actual, on the very right hand of God, can we grasp the Christian claim that all things are to be understood through him. The stormy doctrine of the Second Coming of Christ also indicates an important truth: the closing of the parenthesis of this age. History is precisely parenthetical, and the parentheses are turned outward, not inward.

On the deepest level, the Church *is* one — in Christ, in the Holy Spirit, in the sacrament, in the hope of resurrection. But human sinfulness has divided the historic Church. At the present, three approaches to ecumenical Christianity seem irreconcilable: the literalistic, the liberal, and the sacramentarian. Christianity is a common, continuous commitment to the Holy Spirit who came into the world through Jesus Christ, who activates our individual lives, who expresses himself in the Agape fellowship. But liberal theology is weakened by vagueness; it has no clear principle of exclusion; its tolerance is identical with its lack of intense conviction. As Chesterton put it, "tolerance is the virtue of people who don't believe anything." Traditional theology can keep the substance of its faith, yet accept its intellectual and social responsibility; liberalism can keep its intellectual and social passion, yet recover an adequate and definite standard of faith. By limiting the Christian fellowship to one historic organization, which is clearly but one branch on the Tree of Life, the Roman Church became a sect. No historic organization, whether Italian or North European, has fully incarnated Agape. The apostolic Agape, the Holy Spirit, is the apostolic succession. At times purity of doctrine has replaced papal authority as the end and all of living, but doctrinal idolatry, like papal idolatry, forgets that it is weighed in Love's balances, and found wanting. In Jesus Christ there came into full historical awareness the idea of Christian love, the determinative, distinctive motif of Christianity, its ultimate principle of explanation and its perpetual judgment; in this Light all doctrines are to be defined and understood. Love is normative for Christianity, but Christians have sought to possess, rather than to be possessed by, normative Christianity; they have made of every good means an idolatrous end; the Church has become Roman; the Bible, Presbyterian; and reason and experience, Congregational. In particular, Christianity has succumbed to Christendom, to standpattism and the *status quo*. Atomic Agape has been kept safely under lock and key in the arsenal — under the pulpit or behind the altar.

The Church is the pull of Purpose in history, the magnetism of the Holy Spirit. The push of process itself drives history toward the Church. Even wars demonstrate that history cannot thwart the pulsing power of God's purpose. Willingly or unwillingly, communities become vitally aware of each other. Indifference and ignorance make fellowship impossible; wars make men conscious of each other and of the need for fellowship without which the world cannot survive. What history reveals as man's basic need, Christianity offers as a positive gift. The fellowship which the Church is, and offers through the Holy Spirit, is based not on man's merit, but on forgiving Love. Man's merit divides and damns; God's Love unites and redeems. Agape as faith's final meaning and judgment weds ultimate hope to historic challenge, whereas traditional theology maintains a split universe, an unsolvable dualism, an eternal heaven and an eternal hell. Ferré is certain that a resolute acceptance of Christian love and its application to every sphere of theology and life are clearly on the agenda. Man's relationship to God is neither on the basis of holiness (Aquinas) nor on the basis of sinfulness (Luther), since both are legal and lethal, but on the basis of Love. Agape must be, and is, organically related to all men, all history, and all nature. By the very character of Agape, the works of Christian love, the enterprises of the Church in history, its redemptive efforts in and for every sub-Christian culture that surrounds it, must overflow continuously and increasingly into the whole world, without defensive concern for its acceptance or rejection. Christianity, like Christ, has come, not to destroy, but to fulfill. The struggle between faiths, contrary to Nygren's assertion, is not a struggle to death. Whatever in the different religions of the world is good must be kept and used in the service of Christ by the Spirit.

Ferré hopes that we have now reached the post-Protestant period of Christian history. With Sorokin and Toynbee, he awaits a new age of the spirit, and believes that the present movement is toward a new catholicity which will accept a different form of supernatural-ism yet amply allow for the most cherished values of liberalism. The freedom that liberalism sought from supernaturalism has resulted not a little in relativism, and in many quarters in agnosticism, whether uttered or unexpressed. Liberalism has changed from a negative evangelicalism demanding freedom into an apology for the possession of that freedom. As a historic movement liberalism was man-centered, whereas social history needs to be centered in religion. To have lastingly effective social relations, man needs God. The liberal Church presented a headless body, a fatherless family. Man cannot sustain the burden of his heart without religion, which is simply whole-response to what is regarded as most important and most real. For this reason the world has created and accepted idols; it is dancing wildly, unhappily, and dangerously before the golden calf man has made in his own image. Yet absolutism without liberal-ism is paralysis. Absolutism has fathered asceticism with its unhappy holiness. Liberalism has fathered aestheticism with its unholy happiness. The full Christian Fellowship can and must create and maintain in the Spirit a holy happiness. Only one thing is absolutely certain and never to be questioned, much less denied, namely, that God has revealed himself in Jesus as redemptive Love, that without this Love the world and the Church are lost. When Christianity becomes fully Christian, a new evangelism will explode all barriers and burst forth into the world, positive, earnest, victorious, until the cross of Christ receives its crown, fullness of freedom in fellowship, the glorified Church of God. To confuse the visible churches with the Kingdom of God, or in any way to equate them, is spiritually disastrous. To lose either the absolute or the relative, the eternal or the historical, is to lose the meaning of the incarnation and to forfeit the mystery of God's saving presence in a sinful world. Whenever the hidden God is totally eclipsed by the revealed God, the intensity of religious emotion fades away and we live on diminishing spiritual capital. Without wholesome stress on the otherness of God religion cannot overpower and control the human heart. We must never remove Jesus either from God or from man, yet we are always attempting to do both, to lift him into irrelevance or to lower him into impotence. History — and indeed the churches — exists to be fulfilled in the Church, and the Church, God's Kingdom on earth and in heaven, will never be abrogated or superseded, but only expanded and fulfilled.

It is necessary to understand both the subagapaic actuality of our churches, and the Agape which endlessly creates and sustains the Church within, and beyond, our churches. In Ferré's words:

" In every theological position concerning the Church there is usually a fallacious abstraction, especially since there are at least three inevitable aspects of any adequate doctrine of the Church. The Kingdom of God corresponds to God the Father. Even as he, beyond clear human understanding, is the transcendent source of all ideal embodiment, so the Kingdom of God is the foundational reality of the Christian Church Catholic. This, in turn, may be compared to the Son. Even as the Son is the embodiment of the Father, so the Christian Church Catholic is the extension of the incarnation, of the invisible rule of grace through the succession of saints, of the mystical body of Christ. The Christian Church Corporate, again, corresponds to the Holy Spirit. Even as it, though itself of God, perfect and absolute, works through the media of sinful men and of sinful institutions, so the divided churches represent not only the Kingdom of God, the source of their divine dignity, but also the fallible, sinful conditions of men. Even as the Holy Spirit is Christ with us to the end of the world, the sinless eternal Deity present in our sinful humanity, so the Christian Church Corporate, even in its state of humiliation, is of infinite importance because it is, in spite of the imperfections on its human side, the embodiment of the Church Catholic, the eternal, transcendent Kingdom of God present in the historical flux of human fallibility " (*The Christian Fellowship*, pp. 133, 134. Harper & Brothers, 1940).

Clear is the meaning and the message of the Church; clear also is its responsibility to hallow the earth with grace, to persuade the sons of men to become the sons of God. Christianity is essentially a religion of grace, wherein the natural order of this world is continuously interrupted by the supernatural intervention of God's forgiveness. Through repentance and surrender the self becomes the saint, the divine Agape pours itself into and through him, and fellowship both Godward and manward begins, and never ends. The walls of hell are strong, and they are built from within. The walls of the Church are strong also, and they are built, not from within, but from without.

BEYOND RELIGION
AND
IRRELIGION

The Bridgebuilding Theology of Paul Tillich

The Bridgebuilding Theology
of
Paul Tillich

There appear to be three inexhaustibilities in the universe, in the following order of importance: God, the world, and Paul Tillich. It is not possible to confine him to a single classification; he splits all the categories at their seams. He is Mr. Theology, the theologian's theologian, and is not to be covered in one essay, however thorough, well-intentioned, and long. The human brain vault resembles a nut, and alone among his peers Tillich is a theological nutcracker. There are more things in heaven and earth than are dreamed of in his philosophy, but not many more. He is a philosopher in theology, and a theologian in philosophy; he is a political theorist; he is both historian and prophet — and more; in his intellectual ensemble fact and meaning look well together. His many-sided contribution may be basically characterized as a vast bridgebuilding enterprise; he erects a George Washington span across each of the impassable chasms of modern thought. Without direct dependence upon either Reinhold Niebuhr or Nels F. S. Ferré, he unites the critical theology of the one with the postcritical theology of the other, and transcends both. He unites the ethical dualism of Edwin Lewis with the metaphysical monism of Nels F. S. Ferré, and corrects both. He unites a questioning philosophy and an answering theology in holy wedlock. He unites the Protestant principle with the Catholic faith, transcendence with immanence, Europe with America, liberalism with orthodoxy, atheism with theism, the past with the present, and the present with the future. He ends the comfortable, and sterile, isolation of theology from history, and the uncomfortable and dynamic isolation of history from theology.

To begin with, in the Tillich galaxy of ideas, Christ is the end of the contradiction between religion and irreligion. Neither atheists nor theists are outside of God. Religion is the first burden which Christ takes from the shoulders of men; he gives men the power to overcome religion; his yoke is a New Reality beyond the contradiction between essence and existence, New Life beyond law. Religion is man's heroic attempt to overcome his anxiety; in Christ man discovers that he possesses nothing, not even religion; he discovers that both himself and his anxieties are possessed, grasped, by Unconditioned Love. The strength that sustains the world is stronger than the world, though it is quiet and humble in the world, lest human freedom be annihilated. Jesus is not the creator of another religion, but the victor over religion. In so far as Christianity is one religion, alongside many others, it is blasphemy, idolatry, perversion. One thing only is demanded of man, that he accept his acceptance in Christ, that he receive the life that sustains him from within and from beyond. We call Jesus the Christ, not because he brought a new religion, but because he is the end of religion; the contradiction between religion and irreligion, Christianity and non-Christianity, sacred and secular, is transcended. Divine grace is directly present at every point in history, and to every man in the world, and directly active for man's salvation. One point in the process is no farther from God than any other. Both atheists and theists are grasped alike by immanence and transcendence, yet neither may be identified with the saving power that embraces them. All that exists exists in God, and God is the existence in all that exists, yet God infinitely transcends all finite existence. We are strong only in so far as we point, for our own sake and for the sake of others, to the truth which possesses us, but which we do not possess. Christ accepts our refusal to accept, and thus conquers us. Transcendent Love justifies us in spite of our sins, but also in spite of our doubts. Premature maturity yearns for a Christ of power who will coerce skeptics into faith, but if a Christ of power were to regiment us and our world, we should have to pay the one price we cannot pay, the one price the real Christ will not accept; we should have to surrender our freedom, our humanity, our spiritual dignity. Christ preserves the skeptic's attack upon false religion against all worshipers of the *status quo;* he preserves the skeptic's rejection of all that he does not see as truth; unhurried and unworried Love preserves the skeptic's dignity of refusal. Tillich considers it arrogant and erroneous to divide men by calling some " sinners " and others " righteous." When the righteous do not know that they are sinners, they have added the sin of pride to the sin of separation. The despair of the sinner is closer to the Kingdom than the complacence of the righteous. Sin is the separation of fact from meaning, of immanence from transcendence; sin is from other individuals, from the self, and from God. Yet if man were only separated from God, from other men, and from himself, he would not know that he is separated. In every man, separation is in perpetual tension with union. The righteous share the sinners' separation; when closest to God, men experience most keenly the agony of their estrangement from him. In grace something is indeed overcome; grace occurs " in spite of " something; grace occurs in spite of separation and estrangement. Grace is the reunion of God and man, of man and man, of man and nature, of man and himself, and of the present and the future. Estrangement prevails in nature and in man, in Church and society, in sage and saint. Sin abounds. Man is split within himself. In the picture of Jesus as the Christ, which appeared to Paul at the moment of his greatest separation from other men, from himself, and from God, he found himself accepted though unacceptable. In the knowledge that he was accepted, he was able to accept himself and, as well, every Jew and Gentile. The religious world has always needed, and now needs more than ever, Tillich's rediscovery of the grace that is greater than our sins, but greater also than our theology, greater than either our ecclesiasticism or our skepticism, and greater infinitely than our righteousness. As he sees it, it would be better to refuse God and the Christ and the Bible, and to declare a hundred-year moratorium on all three, than to accept them without the grace that accepts us. We are judged and found wanting; we are rejected; we are sub-Christian, subreligious, and subhuman; the relentless command is upon us all to move forward with singleness of heart toward God's future which endlessly breaks and shakes our present; yet, though unacceptable, we are accepted; though unforgivable, we are forgiven; and the "we" includes all men, Christians and non-Christians, the religious and the irreligious.

Tillich can bridge the impassable gulf between religion and irreligion because he has understood, as few have done, that our knowledge reaches only as far as our uniting love reaches. There is only one way to know another personality — to become united with that personality through love. Full knowledge presupposes full love. God knows me because he loves me; and I shall know him face to face through a similar uniting, which is love and knowledge at the same time. Knowledge that is less than love shall be done away; knowledge shall become eternal in so far as it is one with love. The unpardonable sin of scientists and dogmatists alike is knowledge without love.

Tillich has built several impossible bridges across several impassable chasms, because he is himself a bridge. A direct look at his life discloses that God has made him a span, not only between Germany and America, but also between many controversial philosophies, theologies, political theories, historiographies, and prophecies.

Paul Johannes Tillich was born in Prussia, August 20, 1886, son of the Protestant parson, Johannes, and his wife, Mathilde. The tension between eastern and western Germany was present from the start, for the mother was from the Rhineland, and the father from the Mark. The authoritarian East and the democratic West were united in Paul's birth. The mother's early death determined that the father should be the dominant influence. Classical composure, the son insists, was not part of his heritage.

He was born, and has lived, between two worlds. He is a living illustration that the borderline is the truly propitious place for acquiring knowledge. As Hellenism and Hebraism played irresistible-force-and-immovable-object in Saint Paul, so progressive West and static East collided head-on in Tillich. In his own words: "It has been my fate, in almost every direction, to stand between alternative possibilities of existence, to be completely at home in neither, to take no definite stand against either" (*The Interpretation of History,*

p. 3. Part One tr. by N. A. Rasetzki; Parts Two, Three, and Four tr. by Elsa L. Talmay. Charles Scribner's Sons, 1936). To be a bridge between two temperaments, in his experience, is as unfruitful for decision as it is fruitful for thought. Tillich illustrates the principle that thought is born in conflict; though not a Baptist, he has been totally immersed in inner and outer conflict from first to last. From his point of view, truth dwells not in ivory towers but in the midst of struggle and fate.

Tillich's father was town pastor in the rustic trans-Elbian village; the village itself was barely opening its eyes after the slumber of the Middle Ages. The father was superintendent of the area churches, and as well a functionary in school administration. From his fourth to his fourteenth year Paul loved his uncritical country, yet longed for the critical city. On a journey to Berlin the railroad seemed to him half-mystical. Annual seaside vacations awakened his dreamy appreciation of the boundless ocean as a symbol of the eternal, of the infinite bordering on the finite, erupting into finiteness. This mystical or half-mystical intuition is never absent from the mature Tillich. He sees and describes the fallacy of mysticism, as man's attempt to cross the boundary of finitude, yet his theology remains both mystical and systematic. To him God is always more mystery than meaning, the union of abyss and ground, far and near, "*theos*" and "*logos*," demonic energy and divine purpose. Ferré's view of indirect grace from below and direct grace from above is similar.

Tillich's childhood was a bridge not only between temperaments but also between social classes. He attended the common school, and there acquired a deep animosity toward the upper classes — the burgomaster, the doctor, the large landowners, and his own parents. Later in the Gymnasium, roughly equivalent to an American high school, though distinct in its humanities emphasis, Tillich's real chums were commoners; he felt an increasing distaste for bourgeois youth. He accepted his membership in the privileged class with a painful sense of social guilt. His father was intimate with the old nobility, and the family were often entertained in the manor houses of the squires. The large landowners despised the *bourgeoisie*, Tillich's own class, and, strangely enough, in their feudal tradition possessed some affinity with socialism. The Prussian accent on duty and order provided social and mental stability, but reduced the venture of personal decision. Tillich developed a passionate desire to emerge from every sort of narrowness. His sympathies were with a small antibourgeois Bohemian group, intellectually unconventional, ironically self-critical, and in principle pro-Communist. The common enemy was the anti-intellectual petty *bourgeoisie,* and the Nietzschean aristocratic individual the common ideal.

From his fourteenth to his seventeenth year Tillich struggled with the tension between reality and imagination. External reality was not to be taken seriously; worlds of fantasy were more real. His romantic imagination eventually became philosophic imagination, but his ability to perceive the abstract in concrete imagery remained. He recognized the temptation of the romanticist, to isolate himself from the communal work of science, yet felt profoundly the uncompromising seriousness of prophetic religion. To Tillich, then and now, art is the highest form of play and the unsentimental mirror of the public mind. His father was musician and composer, yet typically Protestant in his contempt for architecture and the fine arts. In Tillich the younger, the love of art turned, in part, to love of literature. Shakespeare, in the Schlegel translation, was important to him, and he identified himself with Hamlet to the danger point. He moved instinctively toward existentialism in philosophy. Goethe, he felt, was not existential enough, and Dostoevsky, the incarnate existentialist, was a late discovery.

In Berlin, on his last furlough as field chaplain in the First World War, he discovered painting through Botticelli; he regards the experience as decisive. The direct encounter produced reflection, with philosophical and theological overtones, and his basic thesis, the necessity of combining cultural form with religious content, came to clarity in his mind. In his view, culture is the form of religion, and religion is the content of culture, and the content, in so far as it is the break-through of revelation, is both form-creating and form-destroying. His belief-ful realism, or self-transcending realism, takes its meaning here. Form must be determined by culture from its own perspective, by its own standards; content must be determined by religion. Into every form must erupt the depth content, the ultimate meaningfulness of the moment. This is the basis of the Tillich trinity of terms, theonomy, heteronomy, and autonomy. Heteronomy makes the tragic mistake of creating its own forms outside and alongside the cultural forms; autonomy makes the tragic mistake of emptying every cultural form of transcendent meaning. Only one world-embracing reality can overcome the schizophrenic split between heteronomous religion and secular autonomy, that is, theonomy — the filling of the cultural forms with religious content, belief-ful realism, or self-transcending realism. In the poetry of Rilke, which his wife, Hannah Werner, later made accessible to him, Tillich discovered again that form both can and must be charged with metaphysical meaning.

Existentialism became Tillich's bridge across the chasm from theory to practice. In his early years it was evident to everyone, and to him, that he was marked out for theory, not for practical activity. He learned from Aristotle's *Nicomachean Ethics* that pure theory alone offers pure happiness; nonetheless he acquired a profound distaste for heteronomous theory, a form of escapism, and dedicated himself to theonomous theory, the uniting of form and content. Neither the Protestant parsonage nor Shakespeare had made him a lighthearted dilettante; both had taught him the first principle of high seriousness: in religious truth the stake is one's own existence; the question is, To be or not to be. To him religious truth is always existential, inseparable from practice. Religious truth is *acted,* in accordance with the Gospel of Saint John. In the creed of the Church, Tillich found transcendent meaning, beyond surface belief and shallow doubt. A man's religion is what he does, because he does what he is; Christ could say, " I am the Truth," and the Church could agree with him, because he taught, enacted, and was Love.

Tillich attended the University of Berlin in 1904 and 1905, the University of Tübingen in 1905, the University of Halle from 1905 to 1907, and returned to the University of Berlin in 1908. In 1911 he received the Doctorate in Philosophy at the University of Breslau. Two years of labor in the Church were followed by four as field chaplain on the Western Front. As an undergraduate he had been a

member, and a director, of *Wingolf,* a student organization that
sought to unite Christian principles with liberal ideas, but he had remained politically indifferent until the war and its aftermath awakened in him a strong sense of social responsibility and a serious hope
for the remaking of the State. Never again was his theology to
retreat from its political task. He entered sympathetically into the
intellectual work of the Social Democratic Party; he became tre-
mendously preoccupied with religious Socialism, and wholeheartedly attacked self-sufficient finitude, the bourgeois spirit; he divorced
himself completely from the separation of heteronomous religion
and social need, and at the same time from a secular socialism which
had emptied itself of religious meaning and was thus bourgeois. In
education, humanistic classicism had been destroyed by scientific
specialization; the universities had become political; by sacrificing
theory to practice they had emptied practice of meaning.

Tillich succeeded in building an important bridge across the bot-
tomless abyss between Lutheranism and Socialism. Calvinism, with
its idea of the Kingdom of God, rationalized at the second generation into a Kingdom of This World, had common ground with
Socialism; this, Lutheranism never had. Indeed, Tillich has never
attempted to build the bridge across the Lutheran-Calvinist chasm.
Nonetheless today he is a member of a denomination that attempts
that engineering feat, the Evangelical and Reformed Church. The
substance of his own religion was, and remains, Lutheran. Lutheranism had erected two barricades against Socialism: religious nationalism and dialectical theology. On German soil religious Socialism
was impossible. Tillich felt then, and has continued to feel, that the
congenital antagonism between religion and Socialism is the tragic
element in German history. The Lutheran view of man is allergic
to all utopian thinking. Tillich found a path through the Lutheran
pessimism in the doctrine of the *kairos,* the possibility of a special
demand and a special expectation at a special historic time. In his
view, the Kingdom of God will always remain transcendent; yet it
is directly related to this world as a judgment against an existing
society and a norm to the next. A decision for Socialism at one time
and place may be a decision for the Kingdom of God, even though

Socialism and the Kingdom of God cannot be equated. Christ, the center of history, is the content of demand and expectation, alike for individual and group, and historic time moves forward irreversibly. Religious Socialism therefore considers capitalism and nationalism demonic, and heteronomous religion profane. Theonomy, which ends the cleavage between heteronomy and autonomy, finds its kindergarten in religious Socialism.

A bridge between idealism and Marxism is to be found in the Tillich epistemology. Hegel did not realize that thinking is entangled with existence, that it is not pure essence. Tillich finds Marx's concept of ideology, the unveiling of sacred and profane self-interest, identical with Luther's idea of the self-made God. In American literature, we have met the same idea in Paul Elmer More's *The Demon of the Absolute*. Where we stand determines what we see, as Kierkegaard discovered in the soul, and Marx in society. Despair is the beginning of hope, for the greatest possibility of obtaining unideological truth is precisely the recognition of present inadequacy. The proof that unideological truth is possible is given in the very statement that many truths are ideologies; if the statement is to be taken seriously it must itself be regarded as unideological. Marx's materialism, as Tillich sees it, was not primarily metaphysical; it was merely a method of historical interpretation, and useful, though negative. Economics involves, but does not exclusively determine, the whole of life in this world; it is therefore fundamental. Both Luther and Marx emphasized that man lives on earth, not in heaven; in existence, not in essence. The unveiling of group ideologies, like the psychoanalytic unveiling of depth drives in the individual, is painful and therefore resisted, yet desperately necessary. Tillich rejects the utopian and dogmatic elements in Marxism, but retains its unveiling technique as truly prophetic. Because he found all political parties distortions, he remained committed to none. Cannot this argument be used with equal legitimacy against membership in our churches? In an age of mediocrity it is hard to criticize Donatist perfectionism, yet is there not sinful pride as well as virtuous perspicacity in purist asceticism? Can it be that perfectionism is itself an ideological cover for the evasion of creative anguish?

Perhaps Tillich's withdrawal from the hazards of party participation is simply a self-restriction of method, a self-limitation of vocation. After all, no human can fight all the battles.

Professionally, Tillich was *Privatdozent* in theology at the University of Berlin, 1919–1924; professor of theology at Marburg, 1924, 1925; University of Dresden, 1925–1929; University of Leipzig, 1928, 1929; and professor of philosophy at the University of Frankfurt-am-Main, 1929–1933. He received the honorary Doctorate in Theology at Halle in 1926. He married Hannah Werner in March, 1924. His book *The Interpretation of History* is dedicated to her. There are two children, Erdmuthe and René.

Partly through the influence of his friend Reinhold Niebuhr, Tillich became, in 1933, professor of philosophical theology at Union Theological Seminary in New York, and began his study, and remarkable mastery, of the difficult tool of a foreign tongue. In 1932, Richard Niebuhr had translated Tillich's 1926 *The Religious Situation* for American readers. Tillich became a naturalized American citizen in 1940, and the same year received the Doctor of Divinity degree at Yale. He was active in the American Democratic German Movement in the closing years of the Second World War. He delivered the Taylor Lectures at Yale in 1935 and the Terry Lectures in 1950. He is a member of the American Academy of Arts and Sciences, and has been both vice-president and president of the American Theological Association. The University of Glasgow gave him the Doctor of Divinity degree *honoris causa* in 1951, and he is the scheduled 1952 Gifford lecturer. He published nine books on philosophy and theology, Protestantism and Socialism, in his native land. Including *The Religious Situation* there are five volumes now available in English: *The Interpretation of History, The Protestant Era* (1948), *The Shaking of the Foundations* (1948), and *Systematic Theology,* Volume One (1951). *The Shaking of the Foundations,* the layman's best introduction to Tillich, contains a series of sermons delivered at Union Seminary and mimeographed in response to student demand before publication. The book uniquely illustrates Tillich's method, and fulfills his purpose, to impart transcendent meaning to the modern skeptic in his own speech. *Systematic The-*

ology, Volume One, correlates the authentic questions from philosophy with the authentic answers from theology; it builds the bridge between reason and revelation in our time; it unites the Protestant principle with the Catholic faith; it classifies Tillich as a twentieth century, and specifically Protestant, Thomas Aquinas. For this study the essential content of Volume Two, in the form of extended mimeographed summaries, was made available. Tillich's view of " The World Situation " (1945) is found in his unique chapter under that title in the worthy volume *The Christian Answer,* edited by Henry P. Van Dusen and produced individually and corporately by the Theological Discussion Group, a meeting of major minds. The society of savants met two week ends each year from 1933 to 1945 to correlate the *kairos,* to relate eternity and modernity, the Christian faith and the social fact. The entire volume unites theology and recent history in belief-ful realism.

Tillich's prolific present is solidly based on his strenuous past. Only through severe struggles with his Prussian father did he achieve the break-through to mental and moral autonomy. Self-assertion as a means of self-discovery, as Nels Ferré has shown, is necessary for everyone, yet Tillich did not lose sight of the inevitable emptiness of mere autonomy. Autonomy filled with religion, this is theonomy for which Tillich crusades. Submission to divine and secular authorities, that is, heteronomy, Tillich has firmly rejected, for his own sake, and for ours, and there is no return. From earliest times he was opposed to the most potent heteronomy, Roman Catholicism, and his opposition was both Protestant and autonomous. At one period, he confesses, he was tempted to surrender to the peace of Rome; for a time it seemed that the only alternatives were national heathenism in Protestant vestments and religious despotism in papal pomp. Both were heteronomies, and both he rejected. His fundamental theological problem is a problem of the bridge: the relation between the absolute and the relative, the Unconditioned and the conditioned, God and human religion. Only an unconditioned God can forgive sins. A conditioned God must defend himself. Beside the unconditioned claim of the divine no other claim can exist. That this claim is established by a finite, historical reality is the root of all heteronomy and of all demonry. The Satanic, the pure evil, exists in theory but not in fact; metaphysical dualism is metaphysical schizophrenia; but the demonic is something finite, something limited, which puts on infinite unlimited dignity — whether Book, person, community, institution, or doctrine. The same demonic distortion has been studied by Nels F. S. Ferré in *Pillars of Faith*. Tillich is certain that Dostoevsky's Grand Inquisitor has entered the vestibule of the German Confessional Church in the strong but tight-fitting armor of Barthian supranaturalism, a new heteronomy, antiautonomous and antihumanistic, the abnegation of the Protestant principle.

In Tillich's words:

" There can be no act of thought without the secret presupposition of its unconditional truth. But this unconditional truth is not in our possession. It is the hidden criterion of every truth that we believe we possess. There is an element of venture and of risk in every statement of truth. Yet we can take this risk in the certainty that this is the only way in which truth can reveal itself to finite and historical beings " (*The Protestant Era*, p. 14. The University of Chicago Press, 1948).

" Protestantism must exist in the constant tension between the sacramental and the prophetic, the constitutive and corrective element. Were both these elements to fall apart, the former would become heteronomous and demonic, the latter empty and skeptical. . . . The question of heteronomy and autonomy has become the question of the final criterion of human existence. . . . In the theonomous, prophetic word, the contradiction of autonomy and heteronomy is overcome. . . .

" I am determined to stand on the border of autonomy and heteronomy, not only principally but also historically. I have concluded to remain on this border, even if the coming period of human history should stand under the emblem of heteronomy " (*The Interpretation of History*, pp. 26, 28, 30).

Not least among the bridges Tillich has engineered crosses the chasm from theology to philosophy. His wish to become a philosopher was formed during his last years in the Gymnasium. And to him the philosophical questions have always been pointless without the theological answers. He could become neither liberal nor orthodox, neither autonomous nor heteronomous. The doctrine of justification, the divine acceptance of the unacceptable, shatters every human finality, every identification of God and man. Yet the same doctrine discloses that human decadence and despair are overcome by the divine acceptance of the sinner and the doubter. For Tillich no approach was possible to liberal dogmatics, which replaced the crucified Christ with the historical Jesus, and dissolved the yes-and-no of justification into moralism.

Perhaps every profound theology must appear Docetic, if only that it may be, in effect, Athanasian. It is, after all, the divinity and not the humanity of Jesus Christ that evoked Peter's confession and ignited the original blaze. To Tillich the foundation of Christian belief is not the historical Jesus; as he sees it, the existence of the historical Jesus cannot be proved beyond doubt; in his view it is possible, though not necessary, to dispense with the historical Jesus; indeed, in so far as the human Jesus has become an idol, rather than an incarnation, he must be dispensed with. Jesus expressly sacrificed all that was Jesus to all that is Christ; the crucifixion, resurrection, and ascension can mean no less. For Tillich, the foundation of Christian belief is the Biblical picture of Jesus as the Christ, not the historical abstraction, a work of the creative imagination. His Docetism therefore may be more appearance than reality: the Christian substance is everywhere present, though presented in a philosophical rather than a Biblical setting. He finds himself against Barth's supranaturalism and for Barth's paradox of justification, and at the same time against liberal dogmatics and for liberalism's historical method. He thinks and lives as both faithful theologian and critical philosopher, and takes care never to lose either dimension in the other. In the First World War and in Nietzsche he experienced the abyss of existence. His philosophy of history is therefore both sociologically oriented and politically formed. He regards metaphysics as a human attempt to express the Unconditioned in rational symbols, but the good word "metaphysics" has fallen into disrepute and is often misunderstood; hence he replaces the word with ontology. To him theology is simply theonomous metaphysics. Tillich appears a complete rationalist; except for other books than his *Systematic Theology* you would never know that he is a committed Christian. However, his rationalism, upon examination, turns out to be only a methodological self-restriction. He is convinced that reason is a critical necessity, that it must be severely exercised despite fanatical resistance, that resistance to reason is heteronomy. In his view reason is basically theonomous; though conditioned by existence, thinking is rooted in the absolute as the foundation and abyss of meaning. The express subject of theology is the assumption of all knowledge, whether or not expressed. From Heidegger, Tillich learned the depth of freedom and the limit of finiteness; Heidegger reached theonomous philosophy through emphatic atheism; he had no answer but he asked the right question, and destroyed heteronomy. Sartre renders a similar service.

Because Tillich, in principle, has ended the war between philosophy and theology, he has, in principle, also ended the war between Church and society. His thinking includes the universe, yet begins and ends at the altar. The Church has always been, and remains, his home. As he puts it:

" I belong to the Church. The years of my youth laid the foundation of this feeling, not only by the Christian attitude of a Protestant parson's home, but also by a rather uninterrupted religious custom of a small city east of the Elbe at the end of the nineteenth century. My love for the church building with its mysticism; my love for the liturgy, singing, and sermon, for the great Church festivals, which for days, even weeks, determined the life of the town; for the mysteries of Church doctrine and their effects upon my spiritual life as a child; the thrilling experience of holiness, of guilt, of forgiveness; the language of the Bible, particularly its pithy sayings — all this together. was effective and created an indestructible foundation of ecclesiastical and sacramental feeling in me. It was decisive in leading me to the decision to become a theologian, and to remain one in spite of all tensions " (*Ibid.*, pp. 41, 42).

His interest in society necessitated his effort to make Church and society one, not through home missions as such, but through religious Socialism; therein alone, in his view, is theological meaning accessible to the proletarian masses. The problem is, in part, one of translation, the necessity of expressing the religious substance in common speech; indeed the entire Tillich theology is an adventure in semantics. The problem is complicated by the fact that there are no substitutes for the original terms. In his view, the only solution is to use the original words, and at the same time to make clear their original meaning, to disavow their secular and distorted usage, to stand between sacred and secular terminologies and interpret the one to the other. Present society has driven many to the sacred-secular border, and precisely there the religious terminology can be heard in its original meaning. When a blind and arrogant orthodoxy monopolizes the ancient words, confuses honest seekers, and drives them into paganism or thrusts them out of the Church, the damage is irreparable and the sin unpardonable.

Finally, Tillich's doctrine of the latent and the manifest Church builds the bridge between religion and culture, and between other religions and Christianity. In every ethical and spiritual religion exists the preparatory Church; indeed, in Christianity itself the Church is often more latent than manifest. He finds secular autonomy often more religious in content than sacred heteronomy. Wherever human existence is subjected to questioning, wherever unconditioned meaning becomes visible in works which have only conditioned meaning in themselves, there culture *is* religious. Sacraments are symbols of the holy; they are not holy in themselves. The Unconditioned alone is holy, and the holy both is and is not in all things at the same time, yet the manifest Church is impossible without a sacramental presentation of the Unconditioned. The latent Church in our secular society can be understood in a pungent Tillich paragraph:

"It will not do to designate as non-Churchly all those who have become alienated from the organized Churches and traditional creeds. My life in these groups for half a generation showed me how much latent Church there is in them: the experience of the finite character of human existence; the quest for the eternal and the unconditioned, an absolute devotion to justice and love; a hope which is more than any utopia; an appreciation of Christian values; and a most delicate apprehension of the ideological misuse of Christianity in the Church and State. It often seemed to me as if the latent Church, which I found in these groups, were a truer Church than the organized Churches, because its members did not assume to be in possession of the truth. Of course, the last few years have shown that only the organized Church is able to carry on the struggle against the pagan attacks on Christianity. The latent Church has neither the religious nor the organized weapons necessary in this struggle, though their use threatens to deepen the chasm between Church and society. A latent Church is a concept belonging to the situation of the border, and it is the fate of countless Protestant men of our day to stand on this border " (*Ibid.,* pp. 48, 49).

If Tillich has one paramount passion, it is that painting, music, poetry, philosophy, and science become at once cultural or autonomous in form, and religious or theonomous in substance. Tillich the bridgebuilding theologian is seen at full stature in his words:

" In face of the Unconditioned, or religiously speaking, of the Majesty of God, there is no preferred sphere, there are no persons, Scriptures, communities, institutions, or actions that are holy in themselves: nor are there any which are in themselves profane. The profane work can possess the quality of holiness, and what is holy can remain profane. . . . It seemed to me that the unconditioned character of religion becomes much more manifest if it erupts out of the profane, disturbing and transforming it. Conversely it seemed to me that the dynamic character of the religious becomes veiled if some institutions and personalities are considered religious in themselves " (*Ibid.,* pp. 51, 52).

THE PROTESTANT PRINCIPLE

To Paul Tillich, Protestantism is an eternal necessity; its essential element would remain if there were no Protestant Churches. He has examined Protestantism continuously for many years, both from the outside, as a student of world history, and from the inside, as a man of faith. He is always a theologian from within the faith, and a philosopher from without. At times he is a philosopher in theology, which accounts for the rationalism of his method and the Docetic quality of his thought. By the same token he is at times a theologian in philosophy. In his view, it is the business of philosophy to ask its own questions, and of theology to provide its own answers; in so far as philosophers have attempted to answer their own questions, and most of them have done so, they have become theologians, whether for good or ill. As he sees it, neither the purely objective nor the purely subjective method can yield the whole truth. Man is subject as well as object; in the study of man therefore the so-called objective approach is the least objective of all, because it is based on an initial dehumanization of its object. The merely objective approach, useful as it is, is especially limited in the study of religion.

Unconcerned detachment, if it is more than a method, becomes a metaphysic; it contains an a priori rejection of the religious demand to be ultimately concerned. It denies the reality of the object at the moment of approaching it. Tillich finds Husserl's descriptive phenomenology useful and necessary; its weakness is that it has no normative principle. For the same reason, Ferré both uses and rejects the Lund theology.

With Tillich's objective method and subjective experience, Protestantism is to be understood as a special historical embodiment of a universally significant principle. This principle, that the divine "No" is spoken against every finite claim of finality, that man is not God, has been demonstrated in all periods of history, in every religion of mankind; it was powerfully pronounced by the Jewish prophets; it is manifest in the picture of Jesus as the Christ; it has been recovered time and again in the life of the Church; it was the sole foundation of the Churches of the Reformation; and it challenges these Churches whenever they leave their foundation. It is the ultimate criterion of all religion and all spiritual experience. Protestantism as a principle is eternal and a permanent criterion of everything temporal. Protestantism as the characteristic of a historical period is temporal and subjected to the eternal Protestant principle. It is judged by its own principle, and this judgment might be a negative one. The Protestant era might come to an end. But if it came to an end, the Protestant principle would not be refuted.

It is the business of theology, in Tillich's view, to discover and apply the Protestant principle, for without it theology cannot perform its necessary work of mediation. The task of theology, as he sees it, is precisely mediation, that is, bridgebuilding, between the eternal criterion of truth as it is manifest in the picture of Jesus as the Christ and the changing human situation. If the mediating task of theology is rejected, theology itself is rejected; for the term "theology" unites the mystery, which is *theos,* with the understanding, which is *logos.* Similarly the Church itself is a bridge between eternal foundation and historical situation; the Church that is not mediation is miscarriage.

Tillich turns the Protestant principle, the basis of mediation, not only against the liberals who lose transcendence in immanence, to whom mediation means surrender, but also against the Barthians, who lose immanence in transcendence and thus make mediation impossible. Dialectics, one of the methods of mediation, seeks the truth through the "Yes" and "No" of debate, until a "Yes" has been reached that unites the necessary differences. In recent years the adjective "dialectical" has been misapplied to a theology that is strongly opposed to all dialectics, all mediation, a theology that consistently reiterates the "Yes" to its own and the "No" to every other position. This misuse of the term "dialectical" has obscured theological movements of a really dialectical, that is, a mediating, character; and it has resulted in a cheap and clumsy division of all theologians into naturalists and supernaturalists, liberals and orthodox. This division is obsolete in the actual work which is done today by every theologian who takes the mediating task seriously.

The Protestant principle is derived from the doctrine of justification by faith: God both rejects man's claim of finality and accepts man. The Protestant principle therefore rejects heteronomy, that is, the doctrine of infallibility, whether papal or Barthian, and at the same time rejects self-complacent autonomy, that is, secular humanism. It demands a self-transcending autonomy, or theonomy. Thus the Protestant principle is the way of mediation, of bridgebuilding.

Not only he who is in sin but also he who is in doubt is justified; indeed only the sinner and the doubter are justifiable, since the recognition of sin and doubt is the recognition of the tentativeness and fallibility of human virtue and human knowledge. Doubt of every human claim is the beginning of faith in the divine claim. Therefore doubt, even doubt about God, need not separate us from God. There is real faith in every serious doubt, namely, faith in the truth which is sought, even if at the moment our only truth is our lack of truth. Truth is divine immanence, and more. If truth is sought as an ultimate concern, the divine is present, though not possessed; the doubter with depth longing is therefore "justified." He who seeks seriously for the truth recognizes that he does not possess it; the fact that he seeks seriously is the proof that it possesses him. He who seriously denies God, affirms him. There is no place *beside* the divine, no possible atheism, no wall between the religious and the nonreligious. The holy embraces both itself and the secular. Being religious is being unconditionally concerned. Neither works of piety nor works of morality nor works of the intellect establish unity with God. Good works do not create divine-human unity; they are created by it. They even prevent it if you try to reach it through them. Unconditional seriousness is the presence of God in the experience of utter separation from him. Faith is the acceptance of one's rejection, and at the same time, the acceptance of one's acceptance. This radical and universal interpretation of the doctrine of justification by faith has made Tillich a conscious Protestant; for him it has meant the conquest of meaninglessness by the awareness of meaning in meaninglessness. No realm of life can exist without relation to something unconditional, to an ultimate concern. Religion, like God, is omnipresent; its presence can be forgotten, neglected, denied. But it is never absent; it is the inexhaustible depth of life, the inexhaustible meaning of every cultural creation.

The Protestant principle makes mediation possible because it makes theology historical. To Tillich, history is the central problem in theology and philosophy because in historical reality he found himself immersed. He discovered historical depth when he returned from the First World War and saw the chaos of Germany and Europe, the end of the nineteenth century bourgeois victory, the split between the churches and the masses, the gap between static transcendence and revolutionary immanence. The situation demanded interpretation as well as action. Tillich found himself and his task, the creation of a theonomous interpretation of history. To him, religion is the substance of culture, and culture is the expression of religion; theonomy and religious Socialism are one.

In Tillich's view a very real barrier exists in the United States to an understanding of the world in which it finds itself a leader. Everything critical of nineteenth century capitalism is denounced as "Red" and, consciously or unconsciously, confused with Russian Communism. Religious Socialism, unlike Russian Communism, is interested in human life as a whole and not in its economic basis exclusively; the exclusive economic interpretation of life, which characterizes capitalism and Communism alike, is empty secularism. Religious Socialism recognizes the dependence of economics on all other social, intellectual, and spiritual factors. Religious Socialism is not a problem of wages, but of a new theonomy in which the question of wages, of social security, is treated in unity with the question of truth, of spiritual security. The stubborn reality of social structures that divorced the masses from meaning meant for Tillich a permanent break with philosophical idealism and theological transcendentalism; both were nonhistorical.

The Protestant principle means not only the critical transcendence of the divine over every conservatism and utopianism, but also the creative omnipresence of the divine in every historical process. Religious Socialism, to Tillich, is not a political party but a spiritual power. It has friends and foes on the Left as well as on the Right. Yet it stands unambiguously against every form of reaction, whether semifeudal and futile as in Germany, the bourgeois *status quo* as in America, or the revived clericalism of postwar Europe. Religious Socialism is not Marxism, though it has learned more from Marx's analysis of bourgeois society than from any other in our time. Tillich finds Marxism much nearer than idealistic theology to the classical Christian view of human nature and human history; Marxism, like Christianity, accents empirical pessimism and eschatological hope.

The Protestant principle cannot be understood merely as criticism of all man-made forms, sacred and secular. Its creativity must also be grasped. God is not only critically transcendent over all heteronomy and autonomy, but he is also creatively omnipresent in every moment of history, and his creative presence is more visible in prepared periods than in others. When the time is ready, the *kairos,* the fulfillment, appears, which overcomes the preparatory contradictions. What happened in the one unique *kairos,* the appearance of Jesus as the Christ, the center of history, may happen in a derived form again and again in the process of time. Christ is the measure of both critical transcendence and creative immanence. *Kairos* is a Biblical concept which could not be used by Catholicism because of its static two-level interpretation of history; and it has not been used by the sects because of their striving toward the final end. Both conservatism and utopianism were, and are, nonhistorical. *Kairos* means that history moves, not in meaningless cycles, but irreversibly in meaningful preparations; hence peak periods, periods of fulfillment, are possible, though never to be equated with the Kingdom. *Kairos* continues the Protestant criticism of Catholic historical absolutism; it prevents the acceptance of any kind of utopian belief, progressivistic or revolutionary; it overcomes Lutheran individualistic transcendentalism; it recovers the revolutionary historical consciousness of early Christianity and the early Reformation; it provides a theonomous foundation for the emergence of the new in history. *Kairos* unites both the criticism and the creativity of the Protestant principle.

The Protestant principle takes seriously both the demonic enslavement and the divine liberation of human freedom. In Tillich's view, the demonic was as real to Luther as to Paul; to both it was the structural and inescapable power of evil greater than the moral power of good will. Theological humanism, as Edwin Lewis also has been at pains to point out, underestimates the power of evil in regarding it merely as an individual's misuse of freedom. The strength of the Lewis position is its recognition of the inevitable dualism of existence; the Lewis limitation is the thrusting of relative dualism upon the ultimate, the finite war upon the infinite. The demonic is precisely the mixture of divine power and human pride in historical institutions and cultures; the demonic has no existence outside history. Both Tillich and Ferré have seen beyond the dualism of immanence the monism of transcendence. Since evil has historical and structural reality limiting individual freedom, its conquest can come only by the opposite, the divine structure, what Tillich calls a " *Gestalt* of grace." To him, the spiritual Church, is a " *Gestalt* of grace " older and larger than the Christian churches. Grace, which transcends history, is also historical, and a continuous war has been, and is now, fought between divine and demonic structures. Aware of its situation at the center of the battle, religious Socialism created its religious, and essentially Protestant, interpretation of history. The strength of the demonic is divine immanence; the weakness of the demonic is divine omnipresence.

Luther's fight with Erasmus illustrates the Protestant view of

grace. We are justified by grace *alone,* because in our relation to God
we are dependent on God, on God alone, and in no way on ourselves; we are grasped by grace, and this is only another way of saying that we have faith. Grace creates the faith through which it is
received. Man does not create faith by will or intellect or emotional
self-surrender. Grace possesses him; it is objectively real, and he may
or may not become aware of it. The interest of early Protestantism
was so egocentric that the idea of a " *Gestalt* of grace " in our total
historical existence could not develop. Indeed, our churches do not
possess grace; grace possesses them, the same grace that possesses the
so-called secular world. Our churches, when spiritually alive, are
witnesses to the grace they do not possess. The Protestant principle
admits no identification of grace with a finite reality, not even with
the visible Church. Without the latent Church, the Church in preparation before, within, and outside Christianity, the manifest Church
could never appear. To build the bridge from the manifest to
the latent Church, and vice versa, is to reunite mankind under the
judgment and mercy of God; this historical bridgebuilding is the
divine enterprise.

Tillich, like Ferré, insists that Protestantism, to be effective, must
become post-Protestant; that is, a profound religious and cultural
transformation of Protestantism is on the agenda. To become post-
Protestant is not to return to papal heteronomy; it is not even, although much more so, to return to early Christianity; nor is it to
surrender to secularism. It is rather to move with self-transcending
realism toward a new form of Christianity, theonomous and world-
embracing, a new *kairos,* to be expected and prepared for, but not
as yet to be named. Christianity is final only in so far as it criticizes
and transforms each of its historical creations; and just this dual
activity is the Protestant principle.

The question may well be asked: How can critical and creative
power be united in historical Protestantism? And Tillich answers:
In the power of the New Being that is manifest in Jesus as the
Christ. Here, in his view, the Protestant protest comes to an end.
Here is the bedrock on which the Protestant house is built to prevail
against hell and heteronomy. To dynamite this rock is insanity and

suicide. Here is the eternal sacramental foundation of the Protestant principle, and the Protestant reality.

Tillich is appalled at the decrease in sacramental thinking and feeling among modern Protestants. Nature has been excluded from religious meaning, from participation in the power of salvation; the body has been disjoined from the spirit. The sacraments have lost their vital power and are vanishing from the Protestant consciousness. The Christ has become Jesus, a religious personality, an example; to the many the Christ is no longer God's union with man, the basic sacramental reality, the New Being. To be sure, Christian leadership must endlessly draw the line between the divine-human mystery and demonic magic, yet the sacrament, the one essential in every religion, is the presence of the divine before our acting and striving, a structure of grace as real as the symbols expressing it. Protestantism has often reduced essential symbols, with their inherent numinous power, to accidental signs; it has therefore tended to replace them with rationalism, moralism, and emotionalism.

Tillich shares and criticizes both the negativism of Niebuhr and the affirmativism of Ferré, though he mentions neither name. As he sees it, cynical realism prevails today, as utopian hope prevailed at an earlier time and now reappears in both Marxian and Ferré eschatology. The Protestant principle judges both cynical realism and utopian hope. It accepts the hope, though rejecting its utopian form; it accepts the realism, though rejecting its cynical form. At this point Tillich and Lewis hold common ground.

An unblinking realism that is full of hope characterizes the Protestant principle. The wars and the revolutions of this century are symptoms of the breakdown of bourgeois liberalism and signs of a coming *kairos,* a radical transformation of Western civilization. On this issue, Tillich, Sorokin, and Toynbee are three men with one idea. In so far as Protestantism is one structure among others in the Western world — and nothing more — it participates in both breakdown and transformation. Not the Protestant era but the Protestant principle is everlasting.

If the Protestant era is to continue in visible form, Protestantism, in the power of its principle, must dissolve its amalgamation with

bourgeois ideology and create a synthesis, in criticism and acceptance, with the revolutionary forces. Protestantism does not now have
but must develop a social ethic determined by the *kairos* under the
judgment of the Protestant principle. The ethic of the *kairos* is the
ethic of love, for love, as Ferré also has emphasized, unites the ultimate criterion with the concrete situation. Because faith and not love
was the be-all and end-all of historic Protestant thought, Protestantism has never sufficiently recognized the centrality of love in Christianity. Puritanism without love is Calvinist, and romanticism without justice is Lutheran. Love, properly understood, is the Protestant
principle, for love criticizes all that is sublove in sacred and secular
society, makes the two worlds one, and creates a new cosmos to replace the old chaos. Primarily, love is not emotional, but ontological.
Love is the essence of life, the dynamic reunion of that which is separated, for separation without reunion is death. Love and theonomy
are one.

Finally, the Protestant principle is the First Commandment. In
Tillich's words:

"It was the Protestant principle that showed orthodox theologians
(both old and new) that the history of religion and culture is a history
of permanent demonic distortions of revelation and idolatrous confusions
of God and man. Therefore, they emphasized and re-emphasized the
First Commandment, the infinite distance between God and man, and
the judgment of the cross over and against all human possibilities. In this
respect also, Protestant theology must be always orthodox, fighting against
conscious and unconscious idolatries and ideologies. . . .

"Man in his very existence is estranged from God, a distorted humanity is our heritage, and no human endeavor and no law of progress can
conquer this situation but only the paradoxical and reconciling act of the
divine self-giving. . . .

"We know three things: we know the Protestant principle, its eternal
significance, and its lasting power in all periods of history. We know,
though only fragmentarily, the next steps that Protestantism must take
in the light of its principle and in view of the present situation of itself
and of the world. And we know that it will take these steps unwillingly,
with many discords, relapses, and frustrations, but forced by a power that
is not its own " (*The Protestant Era,* tr. by James Luther Adams, pp.
xxviii–xxix. The University of Chicago Press, 1948).

THE CATHOLIC FAITH

Tillich the bridgebuilder is at full maturity in the *method of correlation,* basic to his *Systematic Theology.* The sorrow of the past has been either a philosophy exclusively autonomous, or a theology exclusively heteronomous. The method of correlation overcomes the conflict between naturalism and supernaturalism which imperils not only any real progress in theology but also any possible effect of theology upon history. Tillich explores the unexplored: the interdependence between the desperate philosophical questions and the definitive Christian answers.

As Tillich sees it, philosophy, as philosophy, cannot answer ultimate or existential questions. If philosophy offers an answer, the answer is theology, whether good or bad. Conversely, theology cannot answer the philosophical questions without accepting their presuppositions and implications. If logical question and theological answer are separated, the answer is unintelligible and the question unanswered. The questions must not be drawn from the answers, nor the answers from the questions. Philosophy and theology are not separated, and they are not identical, but they are correlated, and their correlation is the problem of Protestant theology. For this reason Tillich is " professor of philosophical theology " at Union Seminary, and Ferré's new professorship at Vanderbilt University bears the same name.

To Tillich neither neo-orthodoxy nor liberalism are valid alternatives. The Protestant principle prohibits old and new orthodoxy, in so far as any orthodoxy regards its truth as final, but also prohibits old and new liberalism which reduces truth to relativism or regards its relativism as absolute. In so far as liberalism is critical of false absolutes, Protestant theology must always be liberal. In so far as orthodoxy keeps as its foundation the Biblical picture of Jesus as the Christ, the center and meaning of history, the criterion of what is or is not Christian, the depth and purpose of life, Protestant theology must always be orthodox. Truth is to be preferred to security, whether liberal or orthodox. The Protestant principle maintains its ground; it looks at Scripture as Holy Scripture, the original docu-

ment of the event, Jesus as the Christ. Theology, to be both adequate
and relevant, must move back and forth between its eternal truth
and the temporal situation. The word "situation" refers not to
psychological or sociological states, but to man's total self-interpre-
tation at a specific period. Fundamentalism and neo-orthodoxy reject this bipolar movement, and thereby miss the meaning of their
task. Kerygmatic theology always needs an apologetic or answering
theology, directed toward the immediate situation, or power shaft
and gears remain apart.

Message and situation are meant for each other. Tillich correlates
the questions implied in the situation with the answers implied in
the message. Half the thinking world evolves questions for which
there are no answers; the other half elaborates answers for which
there are no questions. Tillich rejects both forms of comic theological opera, both forms of futility.

Tillich's method is clear, but his concept, *the theological circle,*
must also be grasped. Every understanding of spiritual things is
circular, that is, it contains a mystical a priori, an awareness of something that transcends the cleavage between subject and object. And
the theologian's working circle is narrower than that of the philosopher of religion. He adds to the mystical a priori the criterion of the
Christian message, the Biblical picture of Jesus as the Christ. The
scientific theologian, in spite of his desire to be a theologian, remains
a philosopher of religion. Or he becomes really a theologian, an inter-
preter of his Church and its claim, and thus enters the theological
circle. He must then admit that he has done so and stop speaking
of himself as a scientific theologian. It is permissible to be both objective and subjective, but it is not permissible to deny it.

In the theological circle, all parts are interdependent. The introduction presupposes both the content and the conclusion, and vice
versa. Tillich's arrangement — epistemology, God, Christ, the Holy
Spirit, and the Kingdom of God — is a matter of expediency for the
sake of the contemporary mind. One can begin anywhere and run the
gamut in either direction. God comes first in both transcendence and
immanence, but Tillich begins with epistemology, because there
man's questions begin. Wherever you start, the theological circle em-

braces the whole of existence and essence. Ultimate concern, without which religion is not religion, is the meaning of the great commandment: The Lord, our God, the Lord is One; and you shall love the Lord your God with *all*. The religious concern is ultimate. All other concerns are conditional. The unconditional concern is total: no part of ourselves or our world is excluded from it; there is no " place " to flee from it. We cannot speak of the " object of religion " without simultaneously denaturing its unconditional character. That which is ultimate gives itself only to the attitude of ultimate concern. The object of theology is what concerns us ultimately. Only those propositions are theological which deal with their object in so far as it can become our ultimate concern. Hence theology does not deal with what concerns us relatively; the theologian is no expert in other fields; he ought never to entangle himself either positively or negatively with preliminary concerns. Our ultimate concern is that which determines our being or not-being. Only those statements are theological which deal with their object in so far as it can become a matter of being or not-being for us. Christian theology is not only theology, but is *the* theology; in its preoccupation with the Biblical picture of Jesus as the Christ, the center and meaning of history, the purpose and goal of process, it is absolutely concrete and absolutely universal at the same time. Philosophy deals with the structure of being in itself; theology deals with the meaning of being for us. In philosophy the place to stand is all places; the place to stand is no place at all; it is pure reason. There is no possible conflict between philosophy and theology, for there is no common basis between them. All conflict rises as conflict in philosophy or as conflict in theology, when the hidden theologian in the philosopher fights with the professed theologian. Thus modern philosophy is not pagan; atheism and anti-Christianity are not pagan; they are anti-Christian in Christian terms.

The Christian claim that the logos that became concrete in Jesus as the Christ is at the same time the universal logos includes the claim that wherever the logos is at work it agrees with the Christian message. No philosophy that is obedient to the universal logos can contradict the concrete logos, " the Logos made flesh." The divine life is the spiritual unity of form and depth, of Logos and abyss. It is the abysmal character of the divine life that makes revelation mysterious; it is the logical character of the divine life that makes revelation rational; it is the spiritual character of the divine life that creates the miracle and the ecstasy in which revelation is received; without the abyss, the divine depth, revelation is information; without the Logos, the divine rationality in which our rationality is rooted, revelation is heteronomous subjection; without the Spirit, which unites mystery with meaning, and both with receptive ecstasy, the experience of revelation is impossible.

The sources of systematic theology are three: the Bible, Church history, and the history of religion and culture. Experience is not a source of revelation, but a medium of reception; it yields insight, but not new material beyond the given in Christ. Insight dissolves every theology that makes experience an independent source rather than a dependent medium. The center and norm of systematic theology is the New Being in Jesus as the Christ understood as our ultimate concern. The partial openness of the Biblical canon safeguards the spirituality of the Church. The Biblical message, Jesus as the Christ, is final, but the Church's interpretation of the message is conditioned by religion and culture, and there is no escape from finitude. The attempt to escape finitude is the religious arrogance which is destroyed, in principle, by the doctrine of justification by faith. Protestants, particularly the neo-orthodox, have inveighed against Roman infallibility, and often substituted their own.

Reason does not, and cannot, create the Christian content; it is a method of examining that content. Reason is not a source of revelation, but a medium of reception. Reason is overpowered, invaded, shaken by the ultimate concern; finite reason is superseded but not annihilated. There is, in the last analysis, only one genuine paradox in the Christian message, the appearance of that which conquers existence under the conditions of existence. Finite man asks about the infinite because he belongs to it, yet the fact that he must ask about it indicates that he is separated from it. Only those who have experienced the shock of transitoriness, the anxiety which is the awareness of finitude, the threat of nonbeing, can understand the notion of

God. Man is precisely the question he asks about himself, before any question has been formulated; the question implied in his finitude is the question implied in universal finitude. The Christian message answers the question of human existence; for the question is man himself. Man's unity with God makes reunion possible; man's separation from God makes reunion necessary. God is the answer to the question, man — man in his essential nature and finitude. Christ is the answer to the question, man — man in his existential self-estrangement. The Spirit is the answer to the question, man — man in whom energy and meaning are separated. Revelation is the answer to the question, man — man whose rationality is finite and enclosed within existence. The Kingdom of God is the answer to the question, man — man who experiences in history the separation of process and purpose. More simply: God is *in* all things that exist; he is the life *in* all that lives. He is *in* the world, but not *of* the world; he is *in* man, but not *of* man. The fact that God is *in* man is the strength of man's reason; the fact that God is not *of* man makes man his own question about God.

Theology begins and ends with God, but Tillich is aware that modern man begins and ends with himself. Tillich meets modern man halfway; he begins with him, but ends with God. He begins with curiosity (epistemology), and ends with the cross and the crown. And he is humble enough to acknowledge that systematic theology is a construct, that revelation is neither given nor received as a system. Nonetheless revelation is not inconsistent. The systematic theologian therefore can interpret the consistency systematically, aware that the self-manifestation of the divine mystery transcends all possible systems, including his own.

The problem, in epistemology, is the relation between the technical reason which reduces ends to means, the ontological reason which reduces means to ends, and the question raised by the existential ambiguity and disharmony of both, the question that is answered by revelation. Every epistemological assertion is implicitly ontological; that is, epistemology does not create ontology, but vice versa; the epistemological preamble is dependent on the whole theological system. The "how" is dependent on the "what," and the

" what " is conditioned by the " how."

Technical reason, separated from ontological reason, dehumanizes man, empties man of meaning, robs process of purpose. Technical reason itself is impoverished and corrupted if it is not continually nourished by ontological reason, and reason without revelation is question without answer. As Tillich sees it, theology cannot accept the support of technical reason in " reasoning " the existence of *a* God. Such a God would belong to the means-ends relationship. He would be less than God. On the other hand, theology is not perturbed by the attack on the Christian message made by technical reason, for these attacks do not reach the level on which religion stands. There is no such thing as *a* God within the context of means-ends relationships. Technical reason is an instrument, and, like every instrument, it can be more or less perfect; as an instrument, no existential problem is involved in its use. The question of purpose involves the ontological reason. In theology one must distinguish not only ontological from technical reason but also ontological reason in its essential perfection from its predicament in existence, life, and history.

Ontological reason enables the mind to grasp and to shape, to receive and to control, reality, for logos, or rationality, is the character of the real. In receiving reasonably, the mind grasps or receives its world; in reacting reasonably, the mind shapes or controls its world. The reasons of the heart are aesthetic and communal, that is, beauty and love; technical reason cannot comprehend them. Being is finite, existence is self-contradictory, and life is ambiguous. Actual reason participates in these limitations. Autonomy means obedience to the law of reason, the logos, which man finds in himself. Heteronomy imposes a strange law; it issues commands from the outside; but this outside is also inside, in the depth of reason. Both autonomy and heteronomy, in knowledge as well as in faith and life, are rooted in theonomy, and without theonomy each goes astray. Theonomy does not mean the acceptance of a divine law imposed on reason by infallibility; it means autonomous reason united with its own depth. There is, of course, no complete theonomy under the conditions of existence. But the quest for it, for a reunion of what is always split in time and space, issues from reason itself; it is therefore not anti-rational. This quest is the quest for revelation. The double fight against an empty autonomy and a destructive heteronomy makes the quest for a new theonomy as urgent today as it was at the end of the ancient world. Totalitarianism without reason and democracy without depth groan and travail together in pain awaiting the City of God. The catastrophe of autonomous reason is complete. Neither autonomy nor heteronomy, isolated and in conflict, can give the answer. Reason does not resist revelation. It asks for revelation, for revelation means the reintegration of reason.

Revelation is the unveiling of the ground of being, of God's presence and purpose in process, for human knowledge. Knowing is a union of the knower and the known; the unity of distance and union, of the far and the near, of the subject and the object, is the ontological problem of knowledge. As Luther put it, God made himself small for us in Christ. In so doing, he left us our freedom and our humanity. He showed us his heart, so that ours hearts could be won. All religious knowledge is knowledge through union with the known, *gnōsis,* as over against *epistēmē,* external knowledge of objects. Knowledge through union is knowledge through ecstasy, and ecstasy is not enthusiasm, but the state of being grasped by the unconditional. That which is not received in ecstasy is a report about the belief in a miracle, not an actual miracle. Ecstasy is the miracle of the mind, and miracle is the ecstasy of reality. Revelation is the unveiling of the depth of reason and the ground of being. It points to the mystery of existence and to our ultimate concern. It is independent of what science and history say about the conditions in which it appears; and it cannot make science and history dependent on itself. No conflict between different dimensions of reality is possible. Reason receives revelation through ecstasy and miracle, but reason is not destroyed by revelation, just as revelation is not emptied by reason.

Historical revelation is revelation *through* history. Indeed history *is* the history of revelation. When the prophets spoke, they spoke about the great deeds of God, transparent events in the history of Israel. When the apostles spoke, they spoke about the great deed of

God, the transparent event that is Jesus, the Christ. There are no revealed doctrines, but there are transparent events that can be described in doctrinal terms. Rationalism replaces revelation with moralism, reminding us of what we already know. It is necessary to transcend rationalism as such with the idea of continuous revelation in the history of the Church, and at the same time to distinguish between the original revelation, the Biblical picture of Jesus as the Christ, and dependent revelation. The original miracle, together with its original reception, Peter's confession of faith, is the permanent point of reference. Original inspiration and dependent illumination are likewise to be distinguished. The divine Spirit, illuminating believers individually and as a group, brings their cognitive reason into revelatory correlation with the event on which Christianity is based. A dependent revelatory situation exists in every moment in which the divine Spirit grasps, shakes, and moves the human spirit. Thus, the marks of revelation, mystery, miracle, and ecstasy, are present in every true prayer. Revelation, whether original or dependent, has revelatory power only for those who participate in it.

There is, in Tillich's view, a possible idolatry immediately related to every revelation, for the bearer of the revelation, rather than the revelation, may become the object of worship. Because Jesus refused to be worshiped, and claimed nothing for himself, but surrendered all that was Jesus to all that is Christ, everything revelatory is present in Christ as the final revelation, and that revelation cannot come to an end.

It is important to realize that knowledge of revelation does not increase our knowledge about nature, history, and man. Research and verification not only can but must be applied severely if additional ordinary knowledge is claimed. If revealed knowledge interfered with ordinary knowledge, it would destroy scientific honesty and methodological humility. Conversely, New Testament philology may contribute much to our understanding of the documents. It can neither contribute to, nor subtract from, the knowledge of revelation mediated through the documents. Ordinary knowledge cannot interfere with knowledge of revelation. No scientific theory is more favorable to the truth of revelation than any other. Galileo and Darwin neither added to nor subtracted from Christian truth. Revealed truth lies in a dimension where it can neither be confirmed nor negated by historiography. Its truth is to be judged by criteria that lie within its own dimension.

Revelation yields many insights into the nature of man, but all are related to what concerns man ultimately, to the ground and meaning of his being. There is no revealed psychology, no revealed historiography, no revealed physics. It is not the task of theology to protect the truth of revelation by attacking Freud or by defending Jung. These systems are more or less successful attempts in the dimension of ordinary knowledge; they are to be judged on their own merits. However, if under the cover of ordinary knowledge matters of ultimate concern are discussed, theology must protect the truth of revelation against attacks from distorted revelations. Similarly, reason must protect ordinary knowledge from extraordinary ignorance masquerading as revelation. This is not a struggle between religion and science, but simply a struggle between true and false revelation on the one hand, or between true and false ordinary knowledge on the other.

From beginning to end Tillich will not allow the permanent basis of Christianity to be relativized. Whether Christianity is true or half-true, Tillich is not prepared to say; he is a man, and not God; he is convinced that Christianity is the substance of Western culture, that a child of Christian culture is a child of Christ, that parenthood is existential, something given and therefore undeniable. For us inescapably Christ is the revelation of our ultimate concern, and therefore to us ultimate. Tillich's five dimensions, epistemology, God, Christ, the Holy Spirit, and the Kingdom of God, are five excursions from one central citadel. He is prepared to defend that citadel against all attacks. In his words:

" There can be no revelation in the history of the Church whose point of reference is not Jesus as the Christ. If another point of reference is sought or accepted, the Christian Church has lost its foundation. Final revelation means more than the last genuine revelation. It means the decisive, fulfilling, unsurpassable revelation, that which is the criterion of all the others. . . .

" The unconditional and universal claim of Christianity is not based on its own superiority over other religions. Christianity, without being final itself, witnesses to the final revelation. Christianity as Christianity is neither final nor universal. But that to which it witnesses is final and universal. . . .

"The appearance of Jesus as the Christ is the decisive constellation of historical forces. It is the ecstatic moment of human history and, therefore, its center, giving meaning to all possible and actual history. The *kairos* which was fulfilled in him is the constellation of final revelation. But it is this only for those who received him as the final revelation. . . . This acceptance is a part of the revelation itself. It is the miracle of the mind which corresponds with the ecstasy of history. . . . Or, it is an ecstasy of the mind which corresponds with the miracle history. . . . The Christ is not the Christ without the Church, and the Church is not the Church without the Christ. . . .

"He stands the double test of finality: uninterrupted unity with the ground of his being and the continuous sacrifice of himself as Jesus to himself as the Christ. . . .

"It would not have been the final revelation if it had not been received as such, and it would lose its character as final revelation if it were not able to make itself available to every group in every place. The history of the preparation and reception of the final revelation can be called the 'history of revelation'" (*Systematic Theology*, I, pp. 132, 133, 134, 136, 137. The University of Chicago Press, 1951).

One must understand further that the final revelation, which judges religion and nonreligion equally, does not deny, but rather confirms, both universal revelation and other religious revelations; by its nature it is the criterion of all revelation. While humanistic theology tends to identify the history of revelation with the history of religion and culture, thus removing the concept of final revelation, neo-orthodox theology and an allied liberal, that is, Ritschlian, theology try to eliminate the history of revelation by identifying revelation with final revelation. The latter group say that there is only *one* revelation, namely, in Jesus the Christ; to which the former group answer that there are revelations everywhere and that none of them is ultimate. In Tillich's view both contentions must be rejected. The final revelation precisely divides the history of revelation into a period of preparation and a period of reception, and this occurs not only in the total historical picture, but also in every culture and in every soul. Missions could have reached no one if there had not been a preparation for the Christian message in universal revelation. Where there is no question, there can be no answer. The period of receiving revelation began with the beginning of the Church. All religions and cultures outside the Church, according to the Christian judgment, are still in the period of preparation. . . . Even more, many groups and individuals within the Christian nations and the Christian Churches are definitely in the stage of preparation. They have never received the message of the final revelation in its meaning and power. Our Churches are not only communities of the New Being; they are also sociological groups immersed in the conflicts of existence. Nonetheless, revelation and salvation are final, complete, and unchangeable with respect to the revealing and saving event; they are preliminary, fragmentary, and changeable with respect to the persons who receive their truth and power. No one can receive revelation except through the divine Spirit and, if someone is grasped by the divine Spirit, the center of his personality is transformed; he has received, though he does not possess, salvation.

Unlike Ferré, Tillich sees the real possibility of loss. The possibility of self-exclusion from existence cannot be eliminated from the revelation. Man lives under the threat of nonbeing, the threat of extinction, the threat of loss of participation in the universe both here and hereafter, the sword of Damocles. Man can exclude himself from both relative and ultimate being. The wrath of God is not something other than his love; wrath is love's rejection of the rejection of love. Saving power is meaningful only under the immediate threat of nonexistence. As long as the condemning function of revelation is experienced, saving power is effective. The absence of saving power is the flight from an ultimate concern, the complacency that ignores both the divine rejection and the divine acceptance. Not to reach the threshold of the Spirit is to die with that which is subject to death.

To Tillich, as to Ferré, the final revelation, and the final salvation, is love, for love conquers the contradiction between heteronomy and autonomy in the concerned soul and the concerned society. Unconcern is death, but concern is the beginning of salvation. The Church is the society of the concerned. As Tillich puts it:

"There is an absolute law which can stand under the criterion of finality because it is not denied in the act of self-sacrifice but rather fulfilled. The law of love is the ultimate law because it is the negation of law; it is absolute because it concerns everything concrete. The paradox of final revelation, overcoming the conflict between absolutism and relativism, is love. The love of Jesus as the Christ, which is the manifestation of the divine love — and only this — embraces everything concrete in self and world. Love is always love; that is its static and absolute side. But love is always dependent on that which is loved, and therefore it is unable to force finite elements on finite existence in the name of an assumed absolute. The absoluteness of love is its power to go into the concrete situation, to discover what is demanded by the predicament of the concrete to which it turns" (*Ibid.*, p. 152).

HISTORY AND HOPE

Tillich both is and is not a detached academician. His is the role of the thinker, but his thoughts grip reality. His Christology tends to be Docetic, but there is nothing Docetic about his attempt to incarnate theology in history. He is at his best as a critic of the present and a prophet of the future. To him, whatever is nonhistorical is nonsense. He is not primarily interested in tracing tendencies within the Churches or even within theology; rather, he is interested in the religious values of secularism, the religious depth in art, science, education, and politics. He is profoundly convinced that present civilization is not only on trial, but has been judged and found wanting; yet he believes that creative forces are at work in the contemporary chaos. He is a theological Diogenes looking for an honest movement. In his view hope is deeper than despair; triumph erupts through tragedy. He crusades against what he believes to be the decaying element in the modern world, the self-sufficient spirit of bourgeois society, characteristic of capitalism and of Communism alike. Compared with his attack upon self-sufficient finitude, the economic revolutions of our time are reactionary. Every revolt against self-sufficient finitude receives his blessing, for the bourgeois spirit seeks human control over nature and mind, has no respect for the given, reduces man from person to thing, end to means, subject to object. He rejoices at the antibourgeois revolt which he finds in art, through Cézanne, Van Gogh, and Gauguin; in literature, through

Strindberg and Nietzsche; in science, through Einstein, Planck, and Bohr; in philosophy, through Bergson, Simmel, and Husserl; in psychology, through Freud and Jung. He profoundly respects early Communism because it was prophetic, and profoundly loathes modern Communism because it is capitalistic. Like Jeremiah, he is set to tear down and destroy self-sufficient *society* to make room for self-transcending *community*. He is a nihilist toward the present and an optimist toward the ultimate.

To him, everything exists in perpetual relation to the Unconditioned, a relation implicit in all life, explicit in religion. His beliefful realism does not idealize or spiritualize what it sees. His skeptical, unromantic, unsentimental attitude accepts what it sees as it sees it. The real is not to be denied, but transcended. In his view, idealism transcendentalizes rather than transcends the real. Faith and realism belong together; idealism evades both. Things as they are never reveal what they are to generalizing analysis but only to sympathetic intuition. All time receives its meaning from its relation to eternity; time is not meaningless but meaning-full; time both is, and can be, invaded by eternity. The eternal invades; it is not tangible and objective. Disciples of the golden age always look to the past; utopianists always look to the future; *kairos* takes the present seriously to transform it. What is not real in our life and thought has neither present nor future. The Last Judgment is the judgment of our time by eternity, and that judgment can be negative, for the demonic power of bourgeois self-sufficiency is too strong to be conquered by either romantic longing or revolutionary striving. Only the true can conquer the false absolute. When the relative masquerades as the ultimate, it provokes a sudden unmasking. Hence socialism and religion not only can, but must, go hand in hand. Socialism without religion is self-sufficiency in sheep's clothing.

Liberalism and Fundamentalism are both nonhistorical and intolerable, alike in their theology and their ethics. Fundamentalism ignores the problem; liberalism ignores the solution. The problem of religious socialism is the reconstruction of Protestantism, the rebuilding of the religious foundation of culture in Europe and America. Both personally and socially religion is a matter of ulti-

mate concern, of the threat of nonexistence, or it is nothing. Tillich
acknowledges with simple honesty that the position from which he
examines the present is a matter of personal decision, that is, of ultimate concern. Every so-called objective interpretation is one part
self-delusion and one part boredom. The shaking of the self-sufficient
spirit, the shaking of time by eternity, is the desperate meaning of
the moment. The present is neither the past nor the future; the present is eternity; that is, it has unconditioned meaning, depth, reality.
To live spiritually is to live in the presence of meaning; without
meaning life is the buzzing of chimeras in the void, " a tale told by
an idiot, full of sound and fury, signifying nothing."

The demonic element of the present is self-sufficient finitude, the
capitalist or bourgeois spirit of Western civilization, with its trinity
of mathematics unrelated to meaning, technique unrelated to *telos*,
and economy unrelated to theonomy. In education, means are substituted for ends; natural sciences have forced humanistic studies off
the highway. In politics, the right and might of the State are placed
at the disposal of the capitalist class for the domination of the proletariat. Protestantism in England, America, Holland, and Western
Germany formed an entangling alliance with capitalism at an early
date, and remains locked in the illicit embrace. Nietzsche the philosopher, Strindberg the poet, and Van Gogh the painter — all three
were broken mentally and spiritually in their revolt against the
bourgeois spirit, its self-assertion and self-sufficiency, its complete loss
of self-transcendence, its divorce of life from source and meaning.
All the tragedy notwithstanding, Tillich sees the eternal as the un-
seen support even of the time that turns against it; solely to redeem
the human spirit from its demonic enslavement, divine grace opens
closed complacence, and brings self-sufficiency to judgment. The recovery of meaning is the shattering of self-sufficiency. The demon-
ridden swine rush madly into the sea, and are drowned, but the
Gadarene demoniac sits quietly at the feet of the Master, clothed and
in his right mind. The mind, as Husserl pointed out, is independent
of the psychical processes in which it actualizes itself. War and revolution have revealed the play of mind upon process, the supremacy
of meaning over mechanics. To some extent, modern catastrophe has

disturbed even the precritical and prespiritual American mind.

The bourgeois rejection of metaphysics is itself metaphysical; it is unconditioned faith in the self-sufficiency of the finite. With the modern breaking of self-sufficiency, the way is open to a new metaphysics of history, to an intuition of the Infinite in the symbols of the finite. In opposition to romanticism, the new metaphysics must be realistic; in opposition to cynicism it must be a *belief-ful realism*. No individual can discover or create the new metaphysics. It is the task of our century and of all mankind. The achievement will enable our time to see itself and its situation in the presence of eternity.

Nowhere in nineteenth century art, with its bourgeois arrogance, does one break through to the eternal; everything presents the metaphysics of a finite which postulates its own infinity. In modern art self-sufficiency is broken. A transcendent world is not depicted as in the art of the ancients, but the reference in things to the mystery beyond them is expressed. The paintings of Jesus in liberal or capitalist Protestantism present a finite being without reference to the eternal. Tillich finds more of the quality of sacredness in a still life by Cézanne or a tree by Van Gogh than in a picture of Jesus by Von Uhde. The continuity of the religious tradition was broken by capitalist culture; the modern consciousness of depth must find itself, without the aid of tradition or symbol, in a pure, mystic immediacy. And this may be done through any symbol. It may even be done through architecture. Not religious buildings, which are dull imitations, but economic structures today reveal something of self-transcendence, the will to break through the limits of finite self-sufficiency.

Art cannot create, but can express, metaphysical meaning. The ultimate is represented in temporal forms primarily through the impermanence and insecurity of the finite. Despair, in modern art and literature, is closer to the Kingdom than complacence. Émile Zola attacked bourgeois self-sufficiency but possessed no self-transcendence. Ibsen was critical of bourgeois complacency but his standards remained bourgeois; only in *Peer Gynt* is the self-sufficient spirit transcended. Stefan George provided the priestly spirit for many but not the prophetic spirit for all. Love and suffering reentered modern literature with Franz Werfel, and even more, with Dostoevsky, whose name is a pseudonym for depth. Two world wars constituted one catastrophe of culture, the unmasking of the demonic character of capitalist society. New Realism, which has uncovered the demonism present in the social world, may, or may not, develop into *belief-ful realism.*

The unconditioned dominance of economic activity chiefly characterizes the bourgeois spirit. Capitalist society began with the emancipation of economics from spiritual and political control; an autonomous economics developed, subject to no law but its own. Free economy tends necessarily toward infinite commercial imperialism. The fast buck and the big buck are the only interests, and infinite expansion in the sphere of the finite the only objective. Infinite expansion exactly describes the self-sufficient finitude which is ever restless but never self-transcending. In the precapitalist era there was a transcendent element in man's relation to things. Property was a symbol of participation in a God-given world. The capitalist spirit has only a dominating, loveless attitude toward things. Personality is first exalted above property, then debased in slavery to mechanics without meaning. Nature, which is raped rather than reverenced, takes a costly revenge. Possessions that have lost their purpose leave the soul naked, empty, and cold.

Secular socialism is a major triumph of the capitalist spirit, a symbol of its strength. Original socialism involved religious eschatology. The capitalist spirit achieved its greatest victory when it took captivity captive, and made its strongest enemy its ally. The transcendent goal of socialism was made finite and temporal. With the loss of religious depth, socialism became bourgeois. Socialist pacifism, for example, is a bourgeois deception; socialism cries " Peace " only in international relations; when class interests are at stake, socialism, like capitalism, unsheathes the sword. Both socialism and capitalism secularize the State, empty it of meaning, make it a mercenary in the class war.

In the practice of medicine the bourgeois spirit substituted means for ends, bodies for spirits; spiritual healing was lost and now struggles to reclaim its essential function through the art of the psychiatrist, the modern shaman or witch doctor. In Tillich's words:

"It must be recalled that with the elimination of the priestly confessional and the loss of its real values the physician stepped upon the scene as a substitute. Yet he was not a substitute who could supply what should have been supplied, a healing process proceeding out of man's central function, that is, out of his religious relations. First of all the separation of body and soul, then the mechanization of the body, then the conception of the psychic as a product of the physical machine. . . . The relation of the physician and patient could only be an external, objective, and contractual relationship, not one of real community supported by love. Such a relationship corresponds to the fundamental lack of community-love in the spirit of capitalist society " (*The Religious Situation,* tr. by H. Richard Niebuhr, pp. 104, 105. Henry Holt & Co., Inc., 1932).

Self-sufficient finitude is the tragedy of the past, but the hope of the future is the shattering of the present. The disintegration and transformation of bourgeois society today holds the center of the stage. The decisive feature of the nineteenth century bourgeois victory was the loss of control by human reason over man's historical existence; the self-destruction of bourgeois society and the complete collapse of the bourgeois scheme of automatic harmony characterize the present transition. Russia leaped from the first to the third stage of social development, from czarism to totalitarianism, from feudalism to futility. In our own land, planning reason has in part replaced technical reason; it is therefore possible, and necessary, to regain some human control over history, to create a society that avoids both totalitarian absolutism and liberal individualism. The great danger is leviathan, a colossal social mechanism erected by finite self-sufficiency. Leviathan, always a quick-change artist, may appear in new garb and continue the deadly dissolution of personality and community. Leviathan is the absolute master of modern education. Education, subjected to the self-sufficient social mechanism, has lost its primary interest in the truth and justice that transcend, and judge, the mechanism. Means have triumphed over ends. The failure in education has opened the modern mind to the standardized mediocrity of radio, movie, press, and fashion; standardized men are all too susceptible to propaganda for old and new totalitarian purposes, old and new standardized meaninglessness. True education enables youth to enter the community of ultimate reality, where humanistic, scientific, and technical elements find cohesive meaning.

In economics, Christianity can and must insist that man's unlimited productive capacity be used for man's advantage; both capacity and advantage are now restricted by the struggle for profit and wasted by the struggle for power. Democracy as a constitutional procedure is a means, not an end; the procedure must not prevent the realization of the purpose; the means must not prevent the end; democracy as an end may necessitate its limitations as a means. Power must be criticized and checked, but power paralyzed is powerless to create democracy as a way of life. Only those political procedures are right which produce and maintain a community where the chronic fear of mass meaninglessness is abolished, where every man creates and shares the self-realization of the community. Bourgeois automatic harmony has not been conspicuously successful in international relations. Christianity inevitably supports world federation — the self-transcendence of sovereign states; the program must begin with a recognition of economic interdependence and the necessity of a common spirit. The alternative is the threat of non-existence that hangs over modern society, a threat perhaps best understood in the aesthetic realm, always the most sensitive spiritual barometer. A panic-driven humanity reveals the onrushing doom in its artistic and poetic creations; modern surrealism and expressionism offer an endless warning of the earthquake.

The breakdown of technical truth has created the longing for existential truth, but existential truth has no criterion beyond immediate fruitfulness for life. Existentialism allows no rational criteria by which to judge its decisions. Existential truth must be reunited with ultimate truth. Early Christianity accomplished this reunion with the *Logos,* the concrete event passionately proclaimed as both existential and universal truth for every man, the specific embodiment of the ultimate rationality. Organized Christianity today represents both adaptation to, and transcendence over, the bourgeois spirit; it is therefore part of the problem to be solved. Religion revolted against papal totalitarianism and prepared the way for self-transcending autonomy, but the autonomy that followed was secularized and self-sufficient. The necessary unity of cult and art can be effected only if the present sacred-secular separation can be overcome. Barth's movement increased the separation; it did not attempt to conquer the Philistine Goliath but rather retired before him. The Churches have not exercised their critical freedom, and secularism has won by default. The Churches in part are mere agencies of the State, the capitalist class, and the *status quo*. To some extent the Churches *have* maintained their spiritual integrity against leviathan; they have remembered in the nick of time that totalitarianism invests its particular loyalty with unconditional validity, that it puts itself in the place of the Church, that it can never tolerate an absolute claim in competition with its own. The Church must recover its sense of mission; it must refuse two cowardly capitulations: to adapt itself to leviathan, and to withdraw from the modern situation; it must fill the form of culture with Christian content.

The Church must remember with gratitude that autonomous reason freed the individual from crippling religious absolutism; at the same time the Church must remember that autonomous reason by itself would have left Christianity without transcendence over bourgeois society. Whatever the cost, the Christian faith must maintain true Christian life against demonic secularism. One method is pietism, but pietism is transcendence without immanence; it accents the true *in spite of* but neglects the true *because of;* another method is moralism, but moralism is immanence without transcendence; it relativizes the Christian foundation. The third method is the " Yes " and " No " which accepts and criticizes every man and every movement at every moment. The third method transcends both pietism and moralism. It makes religion the measure of ethics, rather than the reverse, and stresses that Christian movements and Christian men are denied and affirmed by God at the same time.

Five things, Tillich insists, must be remembered if the Church is to succeed in filling present culture with Christian content. (1) No single thinker or movement can plumb the depths of modernity. (2) The present world situation as a historic fact must be accepted; it is what it is, and can neither be evaded nor avoided. Indeed, the Church must recognize the positive modern contribution, the elevation of reason above authoritarianism and obscurantism. This is a Christian issue whether or not fought in Christian terms. Christian faith which proclaims Christ as *Logos* cannot resist the cleansing role of reason. (3) The Church anticipates no future without tragedy even if the present demonries be conquered. The authentic Christian message is too revolutionary to be utopian, too progressive to believe in automatic progress. (4) There can be no religious escapism. The influences of divine grace must penetrate each historical situation. (5) The Christian answer must unite theory and practice.

Churchmen have heard long lists of their sins, and repentance as well as faith may have come by the hearing. But it is pleasant, honest, and necessary for churchmen to hear upon occasion a list of their virtues. Prophets usually speak the divine " No " to all that is human, both sacred and secular. Indeed the " No " is always present, whether spoken by Amos or Jeremiah, by Niebuhr or Tillich, by Bible or bomb. Tillich the bridgebuilder builds one bridge often neglected, from critical rejection to creative appreciation. In his words:

"Through Christianity's day to day resistance, both theoretical and practical, against the complete domination of technical reason and technical economy over human life, the Church has succeeded in maintaining an authentic spirituality and transcendence. Despite its partial secularization, the Church has profoundly influenced " Christian " nations and secular culture. Its very existence was and is a signpost pointing beyond the mechanism created by man's technical skill and now turned against man's freedom and fulfillment. Through preaching, education, and action, the Churches have exerted a largely subconscious effect upon both masses and individuals. This often unrecognized influence became strikingly visible in the resistance of the Christian masses to the attempts by pagan totalitarianisms to replace Christianity by tribal cults. Moreover, despite the adaptation of the Churches to modern society, they have produced individuals who recognized, exposed, and attacked the system and all Christian subservience to it. The deeper meaning of the present world situation is not unknown to many individuals and groups within the Churches. Indeed, against the nationalistic opposition to the religious and cultural unification of mankind, the Christian Churches have created the Ecumenical Movement uniting Christians of all countries, Christian and non-Christian, enslaved and free. This Movement is the only world unity left in the present demonic disruption of humanity. . . .

"Despite the measure of their bondage to the present world situation, the Christian Churches are the historical group through which the answer must be given " (" The World Situation," in *The Christian Answer,* ed. by Henry P. Van Dusen, pp. 42, 43. Charles Scribner's Sons, 1945).

THE
PERMANENT
REVOLUTION

The Theology of Hope of H. Richard Niebuhr

The Theology of Hope
of
H. Richard Niebuhr

Edwin Lewis stresses the seriousness of the human situation, that man exists in conflict between creative and discreative forces. Reinhold Niebuhr accents human insufficiency, that pride and will to power frustrate and distort man's secular, and religious, life. Nels F. S. Ferré emphasizes divine sufficiency, that man is justified by love. Paul Tillich asserts that neither atheists nor theists exist outside of God, that man is justified by faith beyond doubt and dogma. With H. Richard Niebuhr, American theology makes a distinct discovery, that man is justified by hope. If creativity and discreativity exist from all eternity, on Edwin Lewis' terms, hope is ambiguous. If human pride and will to power are never transcended, on Reinhold Niebuhr's terms, the future is as hopeless as the past. If there is no possibility of failure, on Ferré's terms, hope is unnecessary. Tillich's Docetic Christ (an appearance if not a reality) leaves history with Docetic hope, a depth content which ought to be, but never can be, realized in culture. H. Richard Niebuhr, alone in American theology, understands without utopianism that Christianity is movement and life, a permanent revolution, that the world of culture, man's achievement, exists within the world of grace, God's Kingdom, that culture is therefore convertible, that sovereignty and grace are organically related to every human society and every human soul, that nature and history are perpetually open to redemption. With Edwin Lewis, he is not unaware of the conflict; with Reinhold Niebuhr, he is not unaware that God's future is the critic of man's present. His theology of hope embraces both the Ferré theology of love and the Tillich theology of faith. Ferré's "reflexive superspective" centers in divine pedagogy for the soul; H. Richard Niebuhr's permanent revolution centers in divine pedagogy for society. The needs of society receive Ferré's attention, and the needs of the soul receive H. Richard Niebuhr's attention, but the interest of the one is the pilgrim in community, and the interest of the other is the community of pilgrims. Every present emphasis in American theology is a desperate necessity; it is utopian to underestimate the conflict; it is demonic to underestimate pride and will to power; without love the people perish; if man's Christ does not exceed his grasp, then what is Tillich for? Nonetheless, in this age, like every other age of confusion, crisis, and chaos, while others curse the darkness, a theology is needed which lights the candle of hope, not alone for the future bliss of the saint, but also for the present beatitude of the society of sinners, one family of man plodding along in pain awaiting the manifestation of the Community of Love.

Helmut Richard Niebuhr, clergyman, college president, theologian, was born in Wright City, Missouri, September 3, 1894. From one home have come two major minds, Reinhold and Richard, both representatives of maximum as against minimum Christianity. Between them, though the influence was primarily Reinhold's the two brothers brought to America the Thomas Aquinas of modern Protestantism, Paul Tillich. The Evangelical and Reformed Church is small among the denominations of Israel, yet out of it have come three thinkers to lead the people of God. That two masters of modern theology have come from their home is tribute enough to Gustave and Lydia Niebuhr, the father and mother. Unlike Moses and Aaron, Reinhold and Richard carry equal weight equally well through the wilderness of the West.

H. Richard Niebuhr graduated from Elmhurst College, of the Evangelical and Reformed Church, in 1912, and from Eden Theological Seminary in St. Louis, of the same denomination, in 1915. He received his Master's degree at Washington University in 1917, his Bachelor of Divinity at Yale in 1923, the Doctor of Philosophy at Yale in 1924, and the Doctor of Divinity at Eden. He was married to Florence Marie Mittendorff June 9, 1920. He expresses his gratitude for her advice, encouragement, and practical help in *The Social Sources of Denominationalism* (1929), dedicated to the memory of his father. *The Kingdom of God in America* (1937) is dedicated to Florence and the two children, Cynthia and Richard. He acknowledges in several books an indebtedness to his sister Hulda, and to his brother, Reinhold, " without whose constant interest these pages would scarcely have been written." The critical Reinhold, with fourteen books, is better known; the constructive Richard, with five books, may be better loved.

Ordained to the ministry of the Evangelical and Reformed Church in 1916, Richard was a St. Louis pastor from 1916 to 1918. He was a teacher at Eden Theological Seminary from 1919 to 1922. In 1924, the same year that he received the Ph.D., he began his three-year presidency at Elmhurst College. He returned to Eden Theological Seminary from 1927 to 1931 as professor. From 1931 to 1938 he was associate professor of Christian ethics at Yale Divinity School, and has been full professor at the same institution since 1938. His present title, recently changed, is: Dwight Professor of Theology and Christian Ethics.

His theology of hope, ambiguous at the beginning, slowly matures through books two, three, and four, and is fully formed in the fifth. His first book, *The Social Sources of Denominationalism,* offers more despair than hope; it describes in sad detail the evangelical dismemberment of the body of Christ, the surrender of " one Lord, one faith, one baptism " to nationalist, capitalist, sectional, and racial denominations. Americans can read the book only with repentance and self-examination, for it presents a blow-by-blow account of the scourging of Christ by culture, the triumph of miscarriage over meaning, the Babylonian Captivity of theology to sociology. Whether or not faith determines culture, culture certainly air-conditions faith. The Church may be more than a sociological institution, but not much more. The Church undoubtedly is both divine and human, but its humanity will be grasped with full realism after a patient reading of this historical horror story. So-called secular American history, a perversion of the sacred, can be better understood with the aid of this scholarly analysis. No one-sided view of the divinity of the

Church can withstand this withering fire. A more critical treatment could not be written. The book should be read as a companion to *The Kingdom of God in America,* which presents the other side of the story, internal rather than external history, the living faith behind the grotesque façade of American Christendom. Medieval Christianity centered in the vision of God; Puritans, the seventeenth century founding fathers, were preoccupied with present divine sovereignty; the Great Awakening and the revivals of the eighteenth and nineteenth centuries exalted individual experience of the reign of Christ; the social gospel of the last seventy-five years directed primary attention to the coming Kingdom, but in losing the earlier accents upon sovereignty and grace emptied the Kingdom of meaning. " A God without wrath brought men without sin into a kingdom without judgment through the ministrations of a Christ without a cross." Each bursting forth of the permanent Christian revolution poured its energy white-hot into society; in time each movement cooled in the mold, and shrank into institutions. H. Richard Niebuhr acknowledges in the preface that *The Social Sources of Denominationalism* was one-sided, though necessary, that it failed to explain the reality great enough to endure and survive its own cultural humiliation. Liberals of all shades read *The Social Sources of Denominationalism* with high glee; they pause for reflection in the sequel, *The Kingdom of God in America.*

The two volumes describe the mystery, and the history, of American religion. Between them appeared the symposium, *The Church Against the World* (1935). In the Introduction, entitled " The Question of the Church," editor Niebuhr analyzes the internal and the external threat against the Church, and asks, " What must the Church do to be saved? " Secular culture threatens from without and from within, but the more serious threat comes, not from the world, but from God. In the third section of the book, entitled " Toward the Independence of the Church," Niebuhr urges the liberation of the Church from its bondage to corrupt civilization, a withdrawal preliminary to new battle; he asks no flight from the world, only a purge of worldliness, the divorce of the Church from capitalism, nationalism, syncretism, and anthropocentrism. In his view, only a churchly revolt can lead to the Church's independence; further, there can be no flight out of the captivity of the Church save into the captivity of God. The book included " The Crisis of Religion," by Wilhelm Pauck, and " American Protestantism and the Christian Faith," by Francis P. Miller. Though small in size, the book packs a punch. Read in the context of Niebuhr's later books, it is a stimulating contribution in its own right. Every minister, and every layman who accepts responsibility for the Church, should spend a while with these pages. The title suggests the Christ-against-culture *exclusionism* which Niebuhr later rejects; the content, stressing both withdrawal and return, is closer to Niebuhr's later *conversionism* — Christ the transformer of culture.

The Meaning of Revelation (1941), presented to Douglas Clyde Macintosh and Frank Chamberlain Porter, is an admirable adventure in Christian epistemology. The book describes the inevitable tension between historical relativism and absolute revelation, between external and internal history, between natural religion and historic faith. The problems, as you would expect, are never watered down. To Niebuhr, all our philosophical ideas, religious dogmas, and moral imperatives are historically conditioned; the most prevalent source of error in all thinking, particularly in theology and ethics, is self-defense; the prolific source of evil in life is the absolutizing of the relative, the substitution of religion, revelation, Church, or morality for God. Nonetheless, though both historical object and historical subject are relative, it is often overlooked that the object of study exists to be studied. It is not evident that a conditioned view must doubt the reality of what it sees. In any case, only faith that God exists can speak and think significantly about him. Man as object is infinitely less, and less interesting, than man as subject. Man as object can be known externally; man as subject, to be known at all, must be known internally. Historic faith does not cancel natural religion; neither is it the product of natural religion; it is rather the transformer of natural religion. Christianity, seen from within, since from without it cannot be seen at all, is precisely a permanent revolution, a *metanoia,* which does not come to an end in this world, this life, or this time. In the Christian faith it is understood that man is justified by grace, that God is sovereign, that eternity possesses time. Niebuhr acknowledges in this volume his critical indebtedness to Ernst Troeltsch, and his constructive indebtedness to Karl Barth; he lists also among his creditors Henri Bergson, A. E. Taylor, Martin Buber, Emil Brunner, Paul Tillich (whose 1926 *The Religious Situation* he had translated from the German in 1932), Robert L. Calhoun, and brother Reinhold. The book is basic both to Richard Niebuhr and to Christian theology. Modern men, who pretend an interest in the relation between fact and idea, between thing and word, between science and literature, statistics and selves, external and internal, may wince as they read, but will welcome this book.

The latest book from H. Richard Niebuhr's unhurried mind is by all odds the most valuable. The main problem of *Christ and Culture* (1951) is precisely the problem with which Niebuhr wrestled in *The Social Sources of Denominationalism* and *The Kingdom of God in America,* the tension between Christian commitment and secular involvement. The battle between Christianity and civilization is the main theme also of *The Church Against the World;* the relation between secular and Christian knowledge varies the same theme in *The Meaning of Revelation.* There are, in Niebuhr's view, five definable answers to the question, "What is the Relationship of Christ and the World?" The answers are never found without dilution, yet they are clearly distinguishable in character: the first is *exclusion,* that is, Christ against culture; the second is *accommodation,* that is, Christ both in and of culture; the third is *synthesis,* that is, Christ above culture; the fourth is *dualism,* that is, Christ and culture in paradox; and the fifth is *conversion,* that is, Christ the transformer of culture. The book accepts, supplements, and corrects Troeltsch: to Niebuhr more than to Troeltsch, the relative history of finite men and movements is under the governance of the absolute God; Niebuhr's five types of Christian ethics replace Troeltsch's three. Niebuhr excludes both *exclusion* and *accommodation,* though he acknowledges their positive contributions with care and love. Christianity unrelated to time is either irrelevant or hypocritical; Christianity comfortably domesticated in time is apostasy. The three remaining answers have always dominated the majority of Christian minds. *Synthesis* carefully distinguishes the world of Christ from the world of culture, but conveniently arranges the one above the other in static hierarchy; it thus sanctifies, and possibly petrifies, the *status quo*. *Dualism* places man in unrelievable anguish between the deep blue sea and the devil, between divine holiness and human sinfulness; it thus tends to paralyze action, or serves the State with one hand and the Church with the other, and lets not its right hand know what its left hand does. *Conversion* sees the world of man *within* the world of God, the present endlessly shaken and shaped by God's future, society and man open to revolution and redemption. *Christ and Culture* treats the problem of Church and world, faith and history, more profoundly than Reinhold's 1935 *The Interpretation of Christian Ethics*. The latter volume rejects Fundamentalist *exclusion* and liberal *accommodation,* but fails to distinguish between *synthesis, paradox,* and *conversion,* leaving the problem permanently unsolvable in essential dualism. Richard moves more clearly toward revolution, *conversion,* transformation.

It may not be amiss to point out that Richard, as a writer, is blessed with a sense of humor almost wholly lacking in the published Reinhold; the H. Richard Niebuhr style sparkles with pith and point, with color and fire. Reinhold Niebuhr asserts correctly that a sense of humor is the beginning of prayer; when a man perceives the incongruity of the world, he may next perceive his own; but the treatment is as serious as Reinhold. Outside of *Leaves from the Notebook of a Tamed Cynic,* only one smile can be found in Reinhold's volumes: a footnote quotes a doctor's article in *The New Yorker* declaring that the basic anatomical differences between men and women are here to stay; to this bit of wisdom *The New Yorker* had added, " Goody goody." Neither brother, in fact, has to bow down and worship the other; neither would have time to do so; both are too busy alternately kneeling to God and shouting to men.

THE POINT OF VIEW

To H. Richard Niebuhr, Christian revelation is both normative and descriptive for Christians, descriptive only for everyone else.

When men stop thinking as Christians, they are outside the faith. Christian theology must begin with revelation; men cannot think about God except as believers, who are also historic, communal beings. The theologian must ask what revelation means for Christians, not what it ought to mean for all men. He can pursue his inquiry only by recalling the story of Christian life and by analyzing what Christians see from their limited and relative point of view. Christian theology is inevitably circular; you end where you begin. Yet theology must distinguish original principles from intervening distortions, and on its journey discover the world.

To modern self-sufficient reason, revelation seems simply a device of defense. But reason, standing alone in the universe, cannot account for its own existence; unaware of its own dignity and purpose, it is endlessly prostituted to mercantile ends. Skepticism then turns against reason as well as revelation. Indeed, defensive theology has always created the reactions against it. William Law's defense of the Gospels only furnished new objections to it. Wesley wisely abandoned both the defense of revelation and the attack on reason and preached the gospel. In time the mutual imperialism of reason and revelation may be given up.

Christianity is our history; it can be understood only from its own point of view. No significant political or economic change has ever taken place without a recollection of the past. The modern revival of revelation theology is not due to a conscious effort to resurrect ancient dogma but to the emergence in our time of a problem similar to that with which the classic theologians dealt. Chaos is not an answer but a question. What has made the question about revelation contemporary for Christians is the realization that a man's point of view determines what he sees.

Schleiermacher understood half the problem, the lesser half. In his view, we cannot know God as he is, but only as men experience him. Try as he would to keep God at the center, his thought became essentially and inescapably a theology of experience. Nonetheless modern theology, more than any theology of the past, must take into account that our reason is not only in space-time, but that space-time is in our reason. There is no escape from the dilemma of historical relativism. The space-time situation of the observer must be considered in every case; neither Kant nor Hegel nor anyone else can assume an absolute perspective outside history; if reason is to operate at all it must be content to operate as historical reason. This is no counsel of despair. In our time the recognition of reason's space-time limitation can be for theology in particular, and the social sciences in general, the prelude to faithful critical work. Critical historical theology can, and must, seek an intelligible pattern within Christian history.

Put differently, modern theology should be neither an offensive nor a defensive enterprise; no attempt should be made to prove the superiority of Christian faith to all other faiths; modern theology can only be confessional; it can carry on the work of self-criticism and self-knowledge within the Church. A theology that thus undertakes to understand and criticize the thought and action of the Church is inescapably dependent on the Church for its own criticism. Since it is a social enterprise, it can be neither personal nor private; since it is Christianity's self-analysis, it cannot dwell in some nonchurchly sphere of political or cultural history; its home is the Church; its language is the language of the Church; and with the Church it is directed toward the universal from which it is derived and to which it points.

Historical relativism means relevance to history. Theology must begin with and within Christian history or it has no beginning at all; it is thus forced to begin with revelation, that is, with historic faith. Theology must begin and end with God, but find the world between; it must proceed with confidence in the absolute reality of what it sees from its relative viewpoint; and it must recognize that its assertions about that reality are meaningful only to those who look upon it from the same viewpoint. As Luther understood, God and faith belong together; neither is meaningful without the other. All statements about God made from another point of view than faith are not statements about him at all. All religious faith is unconditionally concerned. Whatever ones heart clings to and relies upon, that is, properly, one's god.

Schleiermacher understood that God is the counterpart of the feel-

ing of absolute dependence. He understood further that it is necessary to keep the feeling of absolute dependence and God together;
otherwise one speaks about the world, not about God. God is always
" my God," or he is not God at all. Nonetheless, Schleiermacher
gradually substituted absolute dependence for God, and thus prepared the way for a faith-centered rather than a God-centered theology, for faithology or religionology instead of theology. The God
of religion became auxiliary; religion was substituted for God. Aestheticism is similarly substituted for beauty, and moralism for virtue.
Ritschl moved outside Christian faith to examine religion, and thus
found its essential element in man over nature, an idea alien to
Christian faith. Christian faith values God as infinitely superior to
man and the source of man's own value; Ritschl valued man's confidence in his own worth as superior to nature. Deity became an instrument, not an end; man became the measure of all things; an
anthropocentric universe was created. Niebuhr believes both Schleiermacher and Ritschl ran into trouble because they attempted piously
to defend religion. Christian faith simply makes the God of Jesus
Christ the measure of all things, and proceeds from there; if it proceeds from anywhere else, it never gets there; if it proceeds from
anywhere else, it is not Christian faith. Nineteenth and twentieth
century churchmen have regarded themselves primarily as members
of national and cultural societies, not as members of the Christian
community; to them therefore Christian faith at best has been only
an auxiliary of civilization. Faith in the God of Jesus Christ is a rare
thing; substitute faiths always wear Christian disguises. Theology
has been taught by many sad experiences that Christian faith is the
only point of view from which the God of Christian faith may be
understood. As Niebuhr puts it:

" Theology may try to maintain the standpoint of Christian faith, that
is, of an interest directed as exclusively as possible to the God of Christian
faith; or it may take the position of faith in some other being, that is, of
an interest directed more or less exclusively toward religion, or toward
the moral consciousness, or toward man's own worth, or toward civilization. When it follows one of these latter interests it does not become more
disinterested and objective than when it takes the point of view of Christian faith; it simply becomes primarily interested in something that

faith in God must regard as too narrow and finite to be a substitute for the father of Jesus Christ" (*The Meaning of Revelation*, pp. 35, 36. The Macmillan Company, 1946).

Even within the Christian faith, one must carefully distinguish between revelation and the God of revelation. Revelation and the "claim of the Christian religion to universal empire over the souls of men" are absolute incompatibles. Christian faith is directed toward God as the only universal sovereign, the one who judges all men, particularly saints, to be sinners wholly unworthy of sovereignty. To substitute the sovereignty of Christianity for divine sovereignty, though it be done by means of revelation, is to fall into new idolatry, to abandon faith in the God of Jesus Christ for faith in religion or revelation. Every effort to deal with revelation must be resolutely confessional. We can state in simple, confessional form what has happened to us in our community, how we came to believe, how we reason about things and what we see from our point of view. A revelation that can be possessed cannot reveal God. The living God possesses us. The revelation that leaves man without defense before God can be dealt with only in confessors' terms. Every Christian confession is a confession of sin as well as of faith, a sinners' rather than a saints' theology.

Christian faith has also its own historical method. The preaching of the Early Church was not an argument for the existence of God, nor an admonition to obey the common human conscience; it was primarily a recital of the great events connected with the historical appearance of Jesus Christ and a confession of what had happened to the community of disciples. As Whitehead understood, religions commit suicide when they find their inspiration in their dogmas. The inspiration of religion lies in the history of religion. Similarly, idealistic and realistic metaphysics, perfectionist and hedonistic ethics, have been poor substitutes for the New Testament, and Churches fed on such nourishment seem subject to "spiritual rickets." The sphere of revelation is internal history, the story of what happened within the living memory of the community.

We cannot say that what we mean can be known if men will but read the Scriptures. We must read the law with the mind of the prophets and the prophets with the mind of Jesus; we must immerse ourselves with Paul in the story of the crucifixion, and read Paul with the aid of the Spirit and the Church. History recorded forward must be read backward through our history. The Bible arose, as form criticism has taught us, out of the life of the Church; hence we cannot know a historical Jesus save as we look at him through and with the community that loved and worshiped him. Neither concentration upon Isaiah and Paul nor detailed examination of their historical situation will enable the observer to see what they saw. One must look *with* them and not *at* them to verify their visions.

History as observed is external; history as lived is internal. Internal history is the domain of subjects rather than objects; it is therefore the domain of faith. In Niebuhr's words:

"An inner history, life's flow as regarded from the point of view of living selves, is always an affair of faith. . . . If man does not see the temporality and futility of the finite he will believe in the finite as worth living for; if he can no longer have faith in the value of the finite he will believe in the infinite or else die. Man as a practical, living being never exists without a god or gods. . . . As a rule men are polytheists. . . . Sometimes they live for Jesus' God, sometimes for country, and sometimes for Yale" (*Ibid.*, p. 77).

To Christian faith, history is both lived and observed; hence Christianity is forever involved in two-world thinking. One-world thinking, whether this-worldliness or otherworldliness, always betrays Christianity into the denial of half its convictions. Observed history alone does not lead to meanings. There is no continuous movement from an objective inquiry into the life of Jesus to a knowledge of him as the Christ who is our Lord. Only a decision of the self, a leap of faith, a *metanoia* or revolution of the mind, can lead from observation to participation, from observed to lived history.

Revelation means that part of our inner history which illuminates the rest of it and which is itself intelligible. As Whitehead saw, rational religion appeals to the direct intuition of special occasions, and to the clarifying power of its concepts for all occasions. The special occasion to which we appeal in the Christian Church is called Jesus

Christ, in whom we see the righteousness of God, his power and wisdom. From that special occasion we derive the concepts that clarify all the events in our history. Revelation means this intelligible event which makes all other events intelligible. The obscurities it explains do not bother men who observe; they distress only men who participate, that is, moral agents and sufferers. It is the heart and not the head that finds its reason in revelation.

The heart must reason; the participating self must seek its own meaning. It cannot make a choice between reason and imagination but only between adequate images and evil imaginations. There is an image neither evil nor inadequate that enables the heart to understand; the event through which that image is given Christians call their revelation.

Niebuhr would have it understood that revelation is no substitute for reason; the illumination it supplies does not excuse the mind from labor; it gives the mind only its first impulse and its first principle. Without revelation reason wanders or serves self-interest; without reason revelation illuminates only itself.

To Christians the revelatory moment is not only an event in their common past. In so far as we are Christians, Jesus Christ is the man through whom the whole of human history becomes our history, and all pasts our past. To remember the human past as our own past is to achieve community with mankind; to remember all denominational histories as our own is to achieve the unity of the Church.

To Niebuhr revelation can substitute no other starting point than Jesus Christ. Benedict and Luther must be interpreted through Christ, and not vice versa. Nevertheless revelation moves; that is, its meaning is realized only in relation to new human situations; revelation makes every moment a drama of divine and human action. The God who revealed himself continues to reveal himself, the one God of all times and places.

Niebuhr insists further that a definition of revelation exclusively in terms of the human Jesus is manifestly inadequate. Unless there is a prior certainty, the value of the human Jesus is tenuous and uncertain. Revelation points to something in Jesus Christ more fundamental and more certain than the human Jesus. Revelation means God, God who discloses himself through our history as our knower, our author, our judge, and our only Saviour. From this point forward we shall listen for the remembered voice in all the sounds that assail our ears; we shall look for the remembered activity in all the actions of our world. The God who reveals himself in Jesus Christ is now trusted and known; he is the contemporary God, active in every event. The story of Jesus' birth, like the story of creation, must be read with God at the center of the story. He met us, not as one forever withdrawn from the world; he is rather the one who acts in and through and upon all things, not as the unconditioned but as the conditioner.

Niebuhr's theology of hope is evident in his non-Barthian view of man. The God who reveals himself in Jesus Christ meets no unresponsive will but the living spirit of men in search of all good. We sought a good to love, and were found by a good that loved us. In a characteristic Niebuhr expression:

" Science cannot abandon its faith in the intelligibility and unity of nature without destroying itself. . . . In dealing with revelation we refer to something in our history to which we always return as containing our first certainty. It is our '*cogito ergo sum*,' though it must be stated in the opposite way as, ' I am being thought, therefore I am,' or ' I am being believed in, therefore I believe.' . . .

" This conversion and permanent revolution of our human religion through Jesus Christ is what we mean by revelation. Revelation is not the development and not the elimination of our natural religion; it is the revolution of the religious life " (*Ibid.*, pp. 140, 190, 191).

THE REVOLUTION IN AMERICA

The divine-humanity of the Church is Richard Niebuhr's constant theme. *The Social Sources of Denominationalism* and *The Kingdom of God in America* must be read in sequence, for the first is a book of despair and the second a book of hope. The earlier volume describes with painful realism the capitalist, nationalist, sectional, and racial dismemberment of American Christianity. The later volume accents the divinity which shines through our dust, the unfaltering faith which began with the sovereignty of God, moved to present personal experience of the reign of Christ, and now looks beyond itself to the coming of the Kingdom.

Fallible humanity and faithful divinity are examined with equal care. When Niebuhr began his study, he realized that the denominations could not be distinguished primarily by their doctrines; the theological approach, by itself, was as bare as Mother Hubbard's cupboard. He was compelled to turn to history, sociology, and ethics to account for the diversity. Christendom, he discovered, has often achieved apparent success by ignoring the precepts of its founder. He learned that it is easier to render unto Caesar the things that are Caesar's if one does not examine too closely the things that are God's. The Churches, he found, have perennially sacrificed the goal of the gospel for the sake of its growth, its *intension* for the sake of its *extension*. Compromise in some degree was inevitable, but compromise unacknowledged was, and is, unforgivable. Denominationalism, in Niebuhr's view, is simply unconfessed hypocrisy, the capitulation of Christianity to nation, class, and color. East, West, South, and North, Slav, Latin, and Teuton, have parted the garment of Christianity among them, and a skeptic world notes with irreverent amusement or reverent despair. The unity of Bethlehem has become the disunity of Bedlam. Pentecost reversed the story of the Tower of Babel; confusion became clarity; yet modern Christendom has reversed Pentecost. Meanwhile the devout devoutly confess, weekly and weakly, " I believe in . . . the holy Catholic Church."

The evil of denominationalism lies in the failure of the Churches to transcend their character as caste organizations. Sects rise of necessity to preach the gospel to the poor. Because the Churches lose faith in the power and practice of the gospel, they adopt the psychologically more effective morale of nation, race, and class; they support the popular morale by persuading it of the nobility of its motives; thus they function as political and class institutions, not as Christian Churches; their principle of differentiation is conformity to social class and caste; their divisions represent the surrender of ethics to economics.

Yet there are beams of light across the shadows, light that makes the shadows darker. The denominational movements develop their

tremendous historical energy only because they are religiously inspired. Religion is their content, social stratification their form. Because the poor are neglected, they reshape Christianity to meet their
needs, and religious discipline quickly lifts them to a new economic
status. Then, impressed by their freshly acquired respectability, they
neglect the new poor. Niebuhr is convinced, with Troeltsch and
Toynbee, that unconditioned religions always begin among the
poor, that all-relativizing religions are the creations of the rich.
Christianity itself began as a religion of the poor. When the new
faith became the religion of the sophisticated, dry rot set in; spon-
taneous energy was lost to studied quibbling; ethical rigorousness
was compromised by the policies of governments and nobilities;
apocalyptic hopes were abandoned as irrelevant to ecclesiastical success.

Protestantism, from the beginning, has been the religion of the
businessman. The Roman Church, despite the failings of scholastics,
popes, and priests, lost its absolute power, not because it did not
meet the needs of the lower classes, but because it did not sense the
needs of the middle classes; it did not accommodate its inflexible
structure to humanism, capitalism, and nationalism. Because Protestantism became middle-class Christianity, the poor were automatically disinherited. Peasant and Protestant were separated by Luther
and Zwingli. American Protestantism, which began with the disinherited of Europe, was for a time unique. The men and women
who found refuge at Plymouth, Niebuhr believes, were true heirs of
the apostles: their piety was simple and fervent, their brotherhood
sincere. But the metal cooled in the mold.

In England, from Diggers to Levelers to Quakers, two ideas were
central: inner experience as the source of authority, and common
hope of the coming of the Kingdom. However, in England and
America alike, the disinherited, once in possession of middle-class
wealth, settled down in the decent bed of middle-class respectability.
They found godliness conducive to economic success, and with success lost godliness. Again, the poor were without a gospel. The time
was ripe for another outbreak of the permanent Christian revolution.
Eighteenth century England was skeptical and indifferent. The

theology of the comfortable produced a brilliant and varied literature, distinguished for sobriety of judgment and elegance of expression, but deficient in depth, unimpassioned, and unimaginative.
The universities were paralyzed by moral and intellectual *rigor
mortis*. Prosperity, which the poor had helped to create but could
not share, flaunted its luxuries in their faces. The fortunate felt that
sense of superiority which flourishes where possession has no relation to merit. Soft religion soothed the well-to-do, and the poor were
cast out. Among the disinherited, Methodism arose. The rich rejected Methodism: it was monstrous to be told that "you have a
heart as sinful as the common wretches that crawl the earth." Un-
fortunately Methodism developed personal rather than social ethics,
was more interested in the vices of the poor than in their economic
status. Because Methodism did not attack social injustice, it was tol-
erated by the complacent and the successful, who could not follow
but were not offended.

As Niebuhr sees it, the character of a religious movement is determined by its definition of sin. To Wesley, sin was vice and laxity,
not greed, oppression, or social maladjustment; to him, sin was
sensuality, not selfishness. Wesley was more offended by the blasphemous use of God's name than by the blasphemous use of God's
creatures. Yet Wesley understood, as in a glass darkly, that when
riches come in at the door, religion flies out of the window: the
form remains, the spirit vanishes. In time Methodism, the religion
of the disinherited, became a respectable servant of the *status quo*.
Niebuhr believes that Methodism was the last great religious revolution of the Christian poor; he considers Marxism, perhaps prematurely, a secular revolution, confusing its form with its content. One
of secularism's chief causes, he finds, is the absence of effective social
idealism within the Christian Churches; they are concerned to redeem men from the hell beyond and hold out little hope for salvation from the various mundane hells in which the poor suffer for
other sins than their own. There is, Niebuhr is convinced, no effective religious movement among the disinherited today; they are
simply outside organized Christianity. Accommodation to capitalism
has been one major factor in the rise of denominationalism, but ac-

commodation to nationalism has been equally potent. As Niebuhr puts it:

" The Churches became nations at prayer, but even in prayer Christians found it difficult to transcend the limitations of national consciousness. The kingdoms of the world became the Kingdom of our Lord and of his Christ, but only by subdividing the latter along the boundaries of the former and by accommodating the rule of the divine Sovereign to the peculiar needs of his various mundane retainers " (*The Social Sources of Denominationalism,* pp. 133, 134. Henry Holt & Co., Inc., 1929).

In America sectionalism, East against West, North against South, immigrant churches with their idolatries of language and culture, and the color line have accounted for their share of disunity. Niebuhr finds that motives are always mixed, that only omniscient psychology is able to determine which psychic source of action is decisive. From a more finite point of view the balance of power between theology and sociology is harder to determine.

Racial division in American Christianity draws Niebuhr's particular scorn. Race discrimination is so respectable in America that it is accepted by the Church without subterfuge of any sort; no theological rationalization is necessary, only the anthropological myth of white superiority. By virtue of the marvelous inconsistency of human reason, racism and the self-evident truth that all men are created free and equal are maintained together. Niebuhr is convinced that the ideal of equality will never be realized until the inferior group, whether women or slaves, asserts itself and compels the Church to translate its principles into practice.

Slaveowners resisted the preaching of the gospel to the blacks on the ground that Christianity made slaves less diligent and less governable, and because a baptized black was automatically exempt from slave status. In general the whites encouraged their slaves' salvation from Satan but not from servitude. The slave gallery inevitably led to black churches. The causes of racial schism are not difficult to determine. Neither theology nor Church policy furnished the occasion for it. The sole source of color denominationalism was social; the Church of Christ was clearly invaded by the alien principle of caste. In Niebuhr's words:

" Something more than a sociological cure seems necessary for the healing of this wound in the body of Christ. The color line has been drawn so incisively by the Church itself that its proclamation of the gospel of brotherhood of Jew and Greek, of bond and free, of white and black has sometimes the sad sound of irony, and sometimes falls upon the ear as unconscious hypocrisy — but sometimes there is in it the bitter cry of repentance " (*Ibid.*, p. 263).

In some degree fellowship has always existed as the Church within the churches. Always there has been some recognition, as Niebuhr puts it, that

" the road to unity is the road of repentance. It demands a resolute turning away from all those loyalties to the lesser values of the self, the denomination, and the nation, which deny the inclusiveness of divine love. It requires that Christians learn to look upon their separate establishments and exclusive creeds with contrition rather than with pride. The road to unity is the road of sacrifice which asks of churches as of individuals that they lose their lives in order that they may find the fulfillment of their better selves. But it is also the road to the eternal values of a Kingdom of God that is among us " (*Ibid.*, p. 284).

Niebuhr has given the sociological air-conditioning of the Christian revolution a thorough factual and historical treatment, but he has not left the subject with a catalogue of the Church's failures. *The Kingdom of God in America* presents Niebuhr's positive interpretation of American Christianity as a dynamic spiritual movement, expressed and suppressed by institutions. He explains that *The Social Sources of Denominationalism* left him dissatisfied. The sociological approach explained why the religious stream flowed in particular channels; it did not account for the force of the stream. Institutions were explained, but not the movement behind and beyond them; the diversity was explained, but not the unity; the culture was described, but not the faith which empowered it. He had appealed to good will to overcome the stubborn inertia of class pride and race prejudice, in the hope that vision would conquer division. This appeal, upon later reflection, seemed wholly inadequate. Yet Niebuhr continues to believe that abstract theology and ethics must always be tested in the laboratory of history.

He began to see that the Kingdom of God was always the dominant idea in American Christianity, as the idea of the vision of God was paramount in medieval faith. The Kingdom of God, however, has meant three distinct things: in early American history the Kingdom meant immediate divine sovereignty; later, it meant personal inward experience of the grace of Christ; more recently it has meant the expectation of the Kingdom on earth, the social gospel. The Kingdom of God on earth without the sovereignty of God and the reign of Christ is meaningless to Niebuhr, yet sovereignty and grace are incomplete without it; neither idea is sufficient alone. The Puritans accented divine sovereignty; the Great Awakening and the revivals stressed the inward reign of Christ; the social gospel moved out to redeem the world but denied its redemptive foundation.

Increasingly Niebuhr is impressed that Christianity can continue its social line of splendor if it remembers not only its goal but also its starting point and the middle of its course. In his view the sovereignty of God and the grace of Jesus Christ must endlessly redeem society. Christianity is primarily neither institution, doctrine, nor ethic, but movement, revolution; it is not static law but dynamic gospel. The true Church is not the organization but the organic movement of those who have been called and sent. Institutions are halting places between journeys. The Franciscan revolution, not the Roman Church; the Reformation, not the Protestant Churches; the Evangelical Revival, not the denominations which conserved and curtailed its fruits, show what Christianity is. Since its goal is the infinite and eternal God, only dynamic movement toward the Ever-transcendent can express its meaning. Similarly, Niebuhr is impressed that Christianity means neither simple progress, either this-worldly or otherworldly, nor static dualism, but constant two-way movement: worship toward God, and work with God toward the redemption of this world.

Christianity's revolutionary and creative strain refuses to be reduced to pattern, yet its universalism must always take on particular historical and relative character, whether in Italy or America, whether in the thirteenth or the twentieth century. The Kingdom of God to which the early Americans were loyal was not simply American culture; it was not political or economic interest exalted and idealized; it was rather a Kingdom prior to America, to which this nation, in politics and economics, was required to conform. The instrumental value of faith for society is dependent upon faith's conviction that it has more than instrumental value; objectivism rather than pragmatism is the first law of knowledge. We must take our stand *within* the movement; *outside* we shall never see what it has seen. Nor can we assume that the critic's standpoint is universal while the object criticized is relative: no relative standpoint is absolute. This-worldliness may seem more objective than otherworldliness to those who have never examined their own presuppositions. When presuppositions are examined, critics become aware that their this-worldly dogma is as much a matter of faith as the dogma of otherworldliness. We must interpret American Christianity on its own terms; we must seek the pattern within it, not superimpose an alien pattern upon it.

Behind early American Christianity was the Reformation, with its fresh insistence upon the present sovereignty and permanent initiative of God. It is God who forgives and saves, not men; it is God who reveals the truth and the life, not human reason. The Roman Church was primarily interested in God's changeless perfection; Luther and Calvin were primarily interested in God's forceful reality, his activity and power — the *regnum dei* rather than the *visio dei*. Early Protestantism never made the free man the starting point either of theology or of ethics. Human freedom was not presupposition but goal. Not the millenarian myth, but the conviction that life is critical and transient, occupied the center of thought.

The dilemma of Protestantism lay precisely in its rejection of absolutism and its need for power. Its denial of all human absolutism made it effective against the Roman political colossus, but ineffective in its effort to replace what it had destroyed. It was strong in destruction, weak in construction. Freedom from religious absolutism left the house swept and clean, but open for occupancy to seven secular demons filthier than the first. Society thought itself emancipated, but was only unbuttoned. How persuade emancipated persons and governments to accept a new discipline? Protestantism, in view of its principle, could have no will to power: supreme power belonged only to God; from every human arrogation of his dominion evil resulted. Catholic critics seemed amply justified in their charge that Protestantism and anarchy were two words for the same thing. The emancipated promptly made themselves absolute. Churches, princes, and businessmen quickly became competing absolutes. The problem of Protestantism, in simplest terms, was this: how live in a divinely governed world which is still corrupt? how give up power and still rule?

The Protestant effort to solve this problem has met impossible alternatives: seeking to escape anarchy it has created new absolutism; reaction against absolutism has created new skepticism. Lutheranism capitulated to the State, Calvinism to Biblical legalism; the sects preached, but could not practice, the separation of Church and State.

The early American Protestants believed that the Kingdom of God was not a society of peace and concord to be established by men of good will; it was rather God's actual rule in nature and in history. His Kingdom was not dependent upon human effort; men and their efforts were dependent upon it; loyalty and obedience meant temporal and eternal welfare. The Pilgrims were nonconformists, dissenters, protesters, independents, only because they desired to be loyal to the government of God: in that positive allegiance they were united, however much their unity was obscured by party quarrels. In result they developed three constructive principles in dealing with necessary power: Christian constitutionalism, based upon the Bible; the independence of the Church from the State; and limitation upon human sovereignty through a system of checks and balances. They did not believe that God belonged to America, but that America belonged to God.

To live under the Kingdom was to live under revelation. Life under the rule of God meant directed revolution rather than safe dwelling in unchanging institutions. As divine determinists, they could no more begin with political construction than economic determinists can begin with religion. Building the independent Church was the first task — not a stable institution once and for all, but free movement Godward and in God's name world-ward. When institutions replace movement, creativity is past. In medieval times Franciscans and Dominicans revolted from secular, institutional Christianity and thus restored the Church; in more recent times Methodist preachers, with their saddlebags and books of discipline, were Franciscans and Dominicans in new apparel. The Great Awakening and the revivals of the eighteenth and nineteenth centuries reasserted dynamism against institutionalism; they also attacked autonomous individualism, for absolute individuals had replaced absolute kings and absolute Churches. Regeneration was badly needed and badly emphasized, for the reconstruction of the individual was accented, and the reconstruction of society excluded. In any case, the movement cooled in the mold. When the revivals went to seed in the later nineteenth century, prudery took the place of promise and power. Emotion, originally released in the redirection of the whole man, ran wild. Bourgeois society held at a distance every influence that might disturb its tight, complacent self-sufficiency; the world was made safe for self-seeking.

Self-sufficient finitude excluded the knowledge of the heart, and with it spiritual insight. To be a member of the Kingdom is to be one who sees the excellency and the beauty of God in Christ, and so loves him with *all* for his own sake alone. Indeed, as Niebuhr defines it, the Kingdom of Christ is the Kingdom of love, and love is not primarily an emotion; it is a tendency to action, or action itself, and practice is the test of its genuineness. Patriotism is not enough; the love of persons is not enough; reverence for life is not enough; love of humanity is not enough. All such love is self-love, though the self be made very large. The Great Awakening and the revivals produced fanatics and lost social vision in individual vision, yet produced great humanitarian activity. As Niebuhr describes the movement:

" There were spiritists among them who made worship an escape, there were activists who used worship only as an instrument if at all, and there were sentimentalists who mistook aesthetic or erotic thrills for the love of God. The essence of the new awakening to the reign of Christ was to be found in none of these, but in faith working by love. . . . For America it was a new beginning; it was our national conversion " (*The Kingdom of God in America,* pp. 118, 119, 126. Willett, Clark & Company, 1937).

However, attention was drawn to the individual's hope of heaven, and society was conceived in static terms. " The happy imprudent were ready to take a chance on the canceled reservations of the saints " (*Ibid.,* p. 135). Social hope slackened. Nonetheless, the idea had been firmly implanted that beyond judgment lay a new world. If the seventeenth was the century of divine sovereignty, and the eighteenth the time of Christ's inward reign, the nineteenth may be called the period of the coming Kingdom. The social gospel is older than 1907 or 1890. William Ellery Channing understood that Christ comes in the conversion, the regeneration, the emancipation of the world. Alexander Campbell conceived of the coming Kingdom in political as well as religious terms. Finney proclaimed that God's Kingdom had come in reconciled hearts, that men converted from self to God must bring forth fruits in social righteousness, that world reformation awaited their obedience. Finney's center of interest was the reign of Christ rather than the coming Kingdom, yet he preached immediate repentance for the sin of slavery and immediate freedom for the slave; his preaching produced many humanitarian enterprises. He understood better than modern social gospelers that the coming Kingdom involves inevitable judgment. Samuel Harris in 1870 taught that redeeming power descends upon humanity from God, and works in human society to redeem it. Gladden and Rauschenbusch believed because they saw — though in a glass darkly — and, seeing, were ready to count all things but loss that they might know the power of Christ's resurrection in the total life of man.

The Kingdom of God in America was precisely a New World symphony. Its weakness lay in the fact that men moved toward social justice without remembrance of their point of departure and without knowledge of their plan of march. Puritanism and Quakerism, the Awakening and the revivals, poured white-hot convictions into the souls of men, only to have these cool into crystallized codes, solidified institutions, petrified creeds. Creeping paralysis extended from Connecticut to the frontier, until every order of American " friars " became a denomination, and every denomination settled down to self-defense. When God's sovereignty is reduced to law and divine-human fellowship to dogma, the dialogue between God and man is dissolved into incompatible doctrine. Man, it is said, is completely determined; man, it is claimed, is free to obey or disobey. What can truly be said of a living process is untrue and unintelligible of the petrified product. The divine Kingdom became an institutional possession, and the permanent revolution a dead memory. It is a familiar picture that Niebuhr paints:

" As the Kingdom of Christ is institutionalized in Church and State the ways of entering it are also defined, mapped, motorized, and equipped with guardrails. Regeneration, the dying to the self and the rising to new life — now apparently sudden, now so slow and painful, so confused, so real, so mixed — becomes conversion which takes place on Sunday morning during the singing of the last hymn or twice a year when the revival preacher comes to town. There is still reality in it for some converts but, following a prescribed pattern for the most part in its inception and progress, the life has gone out of it. It is not so much the road from the temporal to the eternal, from trust in the finite to faith in the infinite, from self-centeredness to God-centeredness, as it is the way into the institutional Church or the company of respectable Christian churchmen who keep the Sabbath, pay their debts promptly, hope for heaven, and are never found drunk either with sensual or with spiritual excitement " (*Ibid.*, pp. 179, 180).

The Great Awakening has become in our century a method for arousing God from slumber. Billy Sundayism, and possibly Billy Grahamism, manipulates mass suggestion. To be reconciled to God now means to be reconciled to the established custom of a more or less Christianized society. In the liberal wing of the Church a God without wrath and a Christ without a cross bring men without sin into a kingdom without judgment. The liberal children of liberal fathers operate with ever diminishing capital. The splendid vision of the transalpine good, of the Kingdom beyond, has faded into the light of common day. Radios have been substituted for golden harps, and motorcars for angels' wings. Heavenly rest is now called leisure. In institutional liberalism as in institutional evangelicalism, the aggressive Kingdom has apparently come to a stop. Yet, Niebuhr insists, institutions can be pregnant sources of new aggression, new breaking forth of water from the rock. There is abroad an unmistakable restlessness, an increasing interest in the great doctrines and traditions of the Christian past, aware that power has been lost because the heritage has been forgotten, aware that there is no way toward the coming Kingdom save the way taken by a sovereign God through the reign of Jesus Christ.

THE COMING KINGDOM

From first page to last in his writing, H. Richard Niebuhr is absorbed with two-world thinking — the dilemma of the serious Christian as he attempts to live a God-centered life in a man-centered culture. He is interested in this problem both personally and professionally; he is himself confronted with the dilemma; and he must find, and interpret, its meaning for others. All his books deal with the agony, and the responsibility, of the Church in the world. And the Church is precisely the community which sees in and through the diverse virtues of Jesus the authority of Christ. Each radical virtue of Jesus may be taken as the key to the understanding of his character and teaching; but each is intelligible only as a relation to God accurately symbolized by no other figure of speech than the one that calls him Son of God.

It is just the authority of Jesus as the Christ that creates the Christian's problem, for this absolute authority impinges upon another absolute, the authority of civilization. Both pagans and Christians find Christ's claims beyond easy reconciliation with the claims of their societies. Christianity itself moves endlessly between Christ and culture; one authority is publicly, the other privately, acknowledged. It is not a problem of liberalism or orthodoxy. However great the variations among Christians in experiencing and describing the authority of Jesus Christ, they have this in common: that Jesus Christ is their authority, and that the one who exercises these various kinds of authority is the same Christ, always identified by his extreme devotion to one God, a devotion uncompromised by the love of any other absolute good. As Niebuhr puts it:

" The power and attraction Jesus Christ exercises over men never comes from him alone, but from him as Son of the Father. It comes from him in his Sonship in a double way, as man living to God and God living with men. Belief in him and loyalty to his cause involves man in the double movement from world to God and from God to world. Even when theologies fail to do justice to this fact, Christians living with Christ in their cultures are aware of it. For they are forever being challenged to abandon all things for the sake of God; and forever being sent back into the world to teach and practice all the things that have been commanded them " (*Christ and Culture*, p. 29. Harper & Brothers, 1951).

The competing authority, which must also be defined, is the total process of human activity, and the total result of such activity, to which now the name *culture,* now the name *civilization,* is applied in common speech. Culture is the artificial, secondary environment that man superimposes on the natural. It comprises language, habits, ideas, beliefs, customs, social organization, inherited artifacts, technical processes, and values. The New Testament writers frequently had this social heritage in mind when they spoke of " the world." The problem is the conflict between the continuity of culture and the discontinuity of Christ, between man's present and God's future. Christ is in but not of culture; he is for the world but not from the world.

Niebuhr wrestles with this dilemma in *The Social Sources of Denominationalism,* in *The Kingdom of God in America,* in *The Church Against the World,* and in *The Meaning of Revelation;* after a lifetime of wrestling, *Christ and Culture* presents both definitive analysis and definitive conclusion. Christians, reading this book, will take their double task more seriously: to live to God, and to be lived by God in the world. In five characteristic ways Christians have sought to solve the problem; the fifth, *conversion,* or transformation, or revolution, is to Niebuhr the most meaningful.

The first solution, *exclusion,* is both necessary and inadequate. From I John through Tertullian to Tolstoy men committed to Christ's authority have attempted to " love not the world." For two reasons, they have never wholly succeeded: they withdrew from the world, but could not withdraw the world from them; the world which was in them went with them into the cloister; more seriously, they could not wholly surrender their assigned task of saving the world. They understood the " in spite of," but not the " because of "; the necessary *withdrawal,* but not the equally necessary *return.* The position is inevitable among churchmen. So long as eternity cannot be domesticated in time, so long as Christ and Belial cannot be united in holy wedlock, so long will the radical solution be attempted. Yet the position affirms in words what it denies in action; men cannot speak or think without language, and language is a cultural achievement. Against the world waiting to be redeemed, *exclusion* builds a high wall. Its attention is focused upon the ultimate, but not the interim; upon the Kingdom of God, but not upon the kingdom of man within it; upon " Thy Kingdom come," but not upon " Thy will be done in earth, as it is heaven."

From Gnosticism through Abelard to Ritschl's " culture-Protestantism," the second solution, *accommodation,* has sought wisely but not well to reconcile the gospel with the science and philosophy of the time. Continuity is emphasized and discontinuity is lost; Christ becomes a hero of culture, the best representative of the human race. Eternity is comfortably at home in time. Christ is an object of veneration, and the noblest authority, but no longer the Lord of heaven and earth. Christ is indistinguishable from the best of culture. He becomes with Hegel and Emerson the founder of a religion of, as well as in, humanity. God and man have in common the task of realizing the Kingdom; and God works within the human community through Christ and through conscience, never upon it from without. Rauschenbusch, Harnack, Garvie, Shailer Mathews, D. C. Macintosh, and Ragaz in Switzerland, usher in the Fatherhood of God and the brotherhood of man. The culture-theology of *accommodation* seems never to understand that man's fundamental situation is conflict, not with nature but with God, that Jesus Christ stands at the center of the conflict as victim and mediator. Yet the acculturation of Christ has profoundly aided the extension of his reign. Culture-Protestants, for example, see that Protestant Fundamentalists always reflect prescientific and dated cultures, that Roman Catholics always identify Christianity with the thirteenth century. Culture has its martyrs as well as the Church; and from their graves have also flowered regenerative movements in society. *Accommodation* has a genuinely pious motive, and in some degree always achieves piously; it takes seriously the necessity of speaking to the cultured among the despisers of religion. *Accommodation* is usually antiprovincial; it understands that the world, not a selected little band of saints, waits to be saved. *Accommodation* perceives the truth, that the otherworldliness of Jesus is always mated with a this-worldly concern; that his future Kingdom reaches into the present. And culture-Protestants are usually preachers of repentance to industrial and political imperialists. There is light in their darkness.

Yet there is also darkness in their light. The offense of Christ's discontinuity with culture and the offense of the cross are removed. Loyalty to culture so far qualifies loyalty to Christ that he is often abandoned in favor of a fragment, an idol called by his name. Extremes meet, and the Christ-of-culture folk are strangely like the Christ-against-culture people: both reject theology with its mediating task; both reject the revelation which transcends its defenders as well as its critics. To the accommodators, revelation is merely rational truth in fabulous clothing for the sake of people with a low I.Q.; or it is merely a religious name for the historical growth of reason. Christianity is all very reasonable to the accommodators, yet it requires one thing that goes beyond reason — the acknowledgment that Jesus is the Christ. This surd remains. Culture-Christians partly recognize that revelation cannot be completely absorbed into the life of reason. Like other men, they encounter the metaphysical surd, the question of existence itself: whether the ultimate is blind and pitiless force, or the Father of Jesus Christ. It is increasingly clear that it is not possible honestly to confess that Jesus is the Christ of culture unless one can confess much more than this.

The one holy Catholic Church, through and in spite of its divisions, has never gone all out for either *exclusion* or *accommodation*. The main body of Christians have tended rather to one or another of the three remaining solutions: *synthesis, paradox,* and *conversion.*

From Justin Martyr to Thomas Aquinas and his followers *synthesis* has recognized the gap between Christ and culture that *accommodation* seldom sees and *exclusion* always widens. To the synthesizers Christ is both Logos and Lord; as Logos he is the reason of God the Creator; hence the form of the world is not alien to him. Yet as Lord he is in conflict with the false content of the form, the corrupt world which claims man's undivided attention apart from God. *Synthesis* considers Greek philosophy the schoolmaster leading men to revelation, Aristotle as Christ's Macedonian John the Baptist. In *synthesis,* Christianity is not against the world, and not accommodated to the world; it has rather accepted full responsibility for the world. Aquinas believes in both Christ and culture; his Christ is far above culture; the highest reach of culture does not grasp Christ. Thomas relates Christ and culture in hierarchy: culture occupies the first floor with science, and the second floor with philosophy, but Christ alone occupies the third floor with revelation, contemplation, and the vision of God. The escalator between the floors moves down but not up. There is a place for everything, and everything is in its place. But movement, dynamism, the endless break-through of grace, from below as well as from above, is almost wholly absent, and the hierarchy itself becomes fixed and final, an idolatrous substitute for God. The wild dance of creation and redemption becomes a stately minuet. The Aquinas *synthesis* makes of the relative an absolute, reduces the infinite to finite form, and crystallizes the dynamic. Life is frozen; cultural conservatism is endemic; *synthesis* underestimates both the demonic and the divine.

All three major solutions are *dualist,* but the second, *paradox,* rejects the *status quo* of *synthesis,* accents the endless battle between irreconcilable opponents. It does not withdraw from the battle with the disciples of *exclusion,* nor deny the existence of the battle with the apostle of *accommodation.* The battle is both real and permanent. Christ is Christ, and culture is culture, and never the twain shall meet; yet every Christian must live forever in both worlds. To the paradoxical dualists, from Paul and Marcion to Luther, man can escape neither sin nor grace. Man is a sinner, and all culture is corrupt. Before the holiness of God there are no significant differences; comparisons between the highest skyscraper and the meanest hovel are meaningless beside the Milky Way. Niebuhr describes man's paradoxical situation thus:

" The sense of sordidness, of shame, dirtiness, and pollution is the affective accompaniment of an objective moral judgment on the nature of the self and its society. Here is man before God, deriving his life from God, being sustained and forgiven by God, being loved and being lived; and this man is engaged in an attack on the One who is his life and his being. He is denying what he must assert in the very act of denial; he is rebelling against the One without whose loyalty he could not even rebel. All human action, all culture, is infected with godlessness, which is the essence of sin. Godlessness appears as the will to live without God, to ignore him, to be one's own source and beginning, to live without being indebted and forgiven, to be independent and secure in oneself, to be godlike in oneself. . . . The hand of power is never wholly disguised by its soft glove of reason. . . . The true dualist continues to live in the tension between mercy and wrath. . . . Living between time and eternity, between wrath and mercy, between culture and Christ, the true Lutheran finds life both tragic and joyful. There is no solution of the dilemma this side of death " (*Ibid.,* pp. 154, 156, 159, 178).

The position of *paradox* is both necessary and inadequate. Its vices and its virtues go together. Its dynamism is itself static; there is no motion forward. The Christian must live forever in unbelievable, unrelievable agony, in unresolvable tension. If there were no practical buffer of worldliness between the dualist's faith and his nerves, he would go insane. He therefore develops a Christian right hand, and a worldly left hand. He places love in God and wrath in the State. Christ's commands, projected into the future, have little to do with the present. Basic in the view is its failure to distinguish between Creation and Fall: to be created is to be fallen; there is no direct relation between God and the world. The Christian must attempt the intrinsically impossible, to hold together two mutual exclusives.

But the virtues of *paradox* must not be overlooked. No human power may be substituted for the divine; all human absolutes are idolatrous usurpations. Further, the dualist sees the unique in the world of grace and the world of law — each has value in its own right. More than any leader before him, Luther understood that precisely in the sphere of culture Christ could and should be followed; more than any other he discerned that the cultural rules were independent of Church law. As a Christian cannot derive medical procedure from the gospel in a case of typhus, so he cannot deduce from the commandment of love police procedure in a commonwealth containing criminals. As there is no way of deriving knowledge from the gospel about what to do as physician, builder, carpenter, or statesman, so there is no way of gaining the right spirit of helpfulness, hopefulness, and humility from any amount of technical or cultural knowledge. If we look to revelation for knowledge of geology, we miss the revelation; if we look to geology for theology, we wind up *on* the rocks. Technique and spirit interpenetrate; as Michelangelo knew, they are not easily distinguished and recombined in a single act of obedience to God. Technique is directed toward the temporal, spirit toward the eternal. Similarly, in human relations, so far as a person is responsible only for himself and his goods, faith makes possible what the gospel demands, that he refuse to defend himself against thieves or borrowers, against tyrants or foes. In so far as he has been entrusted with the care of others, as father or governor, he must use force to defend his neighbors against force.

Kierkegaard was true to Luther; the Christian is to live in absolute relation to the absolute, and in relative relation to the relative. But Kierkegaard's exclusive interest was the individual; he thereby lost altogether the Christian social dimension.

Richard Niebuhr would have us see the permanent relevance of the fifth solution, *conversion*. From the Fourth Gospel to Augustine, Calvin, and F. D. Maurice, *conversion* has involved three basic convictions: (1) since Christ is the Logos of Creation, the world to be redeemed is redeemable; it is neither to be excluded nor neglected; (2) the Fall of man is man's action, not God's; man's Fall is therefore moral and personal, not metaphysical; man's nature is misdirected good, not evil; the world is perverted good, not evil; the goal of nature and man is therefore not destruction but redemption; and (3) with God all things are possible in history, for history is a drama between God and men; the Christian is therefore not to live between the times but in the divine now, the eschatological present. Eternity is the presence of God in time, a quality of existence. God sent not his Son into culture to condemn culture, but that culture through him might be saved.

The theme of the Fourth Gospel, Niebuhr finds, is primarily *conversion,* secondarily *exclusion.* The Fall is perversion of created good; sin is the denial of the principle of life; both Creation and Fall are *present;* new life is the beginning with God in the spirit; the Paraclete replaces the Second Coming. John's interest is the spiritual transformation of man's life in the world, not the substitution of a spiritual for a temporal existence, nor the replacement of the physical by a metaphysical body, nor the gradual ascent from the temporal to the eternal. The flesh profits nothing; neither its beginning nor its ending is significant. For the writer of the Fourth Gospel, the Christian life is converted cultural life, life proceeding from the regeneration of man's spirit, but the elect community is the focus of interest. The rebirth of the spirit of all men and the transformation of all cultural existence by the incarnate Word, the risen Lord, and the life-giving Paraclete do not enter into his vision. He has combined *conversion* with *exclusion.*

With Augustine and other Christian revolutionaries, the Roman Empire was converted from a Caesar-centered community into medieval Christendom. To Augustine, Christ redirects, reinvigorates, and regenerates the total life of man; the new life expresses itself in all man's cultural creations. Present culture is the perverted and corrupt expression of a fundamentally good nature. In Niebuhr's words:

" To mankind with this perverted nature and corrupted culture Jesus Christ has come to heal and renew what sin has infected with the sickness unto death. By his life and his death he makes plain to man the greatness of God's love and the depth of human sin; by revelation and instruction he reattaches the soul to God, the source of its being and goodness, and restores it to the right order of love, causing it to love whatever it loves in God and not in the context of selfishness or of idolatrous devotion to the creature " (*Ibid.,* p. 213).

Augustine began with universal *conversion,* but eventually developed *exclusion,* and passed both along to Calvin. To Augustine, the alpha, and to Calvin, the omega, of the medieval Church, the elect exclude and do not redeem the world; they do not give rise to a new humanity; they save themselves — others they cannot save. The

Christian religion, a cultural achievement, is substituted for Christ. Defensiveness, not God, is the author of *exclusion:* the God who chose *all* men for life became the God who chose *some* men for death. Hell and heaven were separated, and both catapulted into eternity.

To John Wesley and to F. D. Maurice, Christ was the transformer of life. Things that are impossible with men are possible with God. There can be some present fulfillment of the promise. Man in time can become a child of eternity, though Wesley, like Kierkegaard, thought in individual, not in social, terms. Wesley's movement, however, was more profound than its modern offspring: on the one hand Methodism has developed the psychological mechanics of shabby revivalism, with mass production of renovated souls, and on the other salvation by sociology. Methodism at times has capitulated to a spurious social gospel which expects " to change prodigal mankind by improving the quality of the husks served in the pigsty."

F. D. Maurice, almost alone in his generation, understood that the Christ who came into the world came unto his own, that Christ himself exercises his kinship over men, not a viceregent — whether pope, Scriptures, Christian religion, Church, or inner light. Every man is in Christ, and Christ is in every man. Christ is Lord of all *now.* Some men disbelieve and walk after the flesh; some men believe and walk after the Spirit; but all men are in Christ. Maurice attacked with equal fervor both unsocial Christians and unchristian socialists. To him, the heresy of our age is religion against God, and Christianity against Christ. In his view, the abyss of love is deeper than the abyss of hate. He preached the participation of all organizations and nationalities in Christ's universal Kingdom. Man is not Christ; man is an unbeliever and a sinner; yet Christ remains the head of every man. The Christian's task is to realize with humility that he is not the head, and with exaltation accept his assignment from the head. Maurice was not opposed to cultural variety: variety brings disorder only because men mistake their partial truths for the whole truth; Christian transformation, *conversion,* revolution occur when humility and service replace self-assertion and self-glorification. Christ's Kingdom is both actuality and possibility. Eternity is not a dimension of time, but a dimension of divine action upon time. The point is not human progress in culture, but the divine *conversion* of the spirit of man from which all culture rises. Every moment, every period, is the eschatological present, the invasion of time by eternity; in every moment men are dealing positively or negatively with God.

Whether the individual adopts *exclusion, accommodation, synthesis, paradox,* or *conversion,* his conclusion is not an abstraction but a decision. Richard Niebuhr lists the many writers who have helped him to " seine out of the sea of history " the typical answers: John Baillie, Karl Barth, Nicolas Berdyaev, Emil Brunner, Charles Norris Cochrane, Christopher Dawson, T. S. Eliot, Jacques Maritain, Reinhold Niebuhr, Paul Tillich, and Arnold Toynbee. From his point of view no single conclusion can be " the Christian answer." The claim of finality by any finite mind, with limited and little faith, usurps the Lordship of Christ; at the same time it violates the liberty of Christian men and the unconcluded history of their culture. Nonetheless each man must decide; every man is responsible to reach conclusions in present decisions and present obedience. For four reasons our conclusions are relative: our knowledge is fragmentary; our faith is feeble; our perspectives are partial; and we often give first-class allegiance to second-class values. We need continually to be reminded that science is no substitute for morals, but also that morals are no substitute for science. Humility and hope look well together in Niebuhr's words: " There is perhaps a little Christianity in our answer " (*Ibid.,* p. 236).

In his view, we are not farther from Christ because we live nineteen and a half centuries after Jesus' birth than disciples in the thirteenth or the first century. Necessarily we see Christ against our own background; we hear his words as particular men in particular times with particular duties. We are relative men; with relative viewpoints, relative evaluations, and relative values, we make our decisions. We are not free not to choose; rather, we are forced to decide whether we will choose with reasoning faithlessness or with reasoning faith. As Niebuhr puts it:

" If we have no faith in the absolute faithfulness of God-in-Christ, it will doubtless be difficult for us to discern the relativity of our faith. Because that faith is weak, therefore we shall always endeavor to make our personal or our social faith into an absolute. But with the little faith we have in the faithfulness of God, we can make the decisions of little faith with some confidence, and with reliance on the forgiveness of the sin that is involved in our action. . . .

" The present moment is the time of decision; and the meaning of the present is that it is the time dimension of freedom and decision. . . .

" Our decisions must be made in the present moment — but in the presence of historical beings whose history has been made sacred by the historical, remembered actions of the one who inhabits eternity. . . .

" We do not trust the God of faith because we believe that certain writings are trustworthy. Yet it is our conviction that God is faithful, that we can say ' Our Father ' to that which has elected us to live, to die, and to inherit life beyond life. Faithfulness is the moral reason in all things. Yet without the historic incarnation of that faith in Jesus Christ we should be lost in faithlessness. He is simply there with his faith and with his creation of faith. . . .

" The world of culture, man's achievement, exists within the world of grace, God's Kingdom " (*Ibid.,* pp. 239, 246, 249, 255, 256).

A WORLD
IN
THE MAKING

The Theology of Work of Robert L. Calhoun

The Theology of Work
of
Robert L. Calhoun

The trend in our time is evident in the name given by Paul Tillich and Nels F. S. Ferré to their departments at Union and Vanderbilt — "Philosophical Theology." Theology is everywhere rediscovering both its inner integrity and its essential relation to modern history and modern thought. The distinctiveness of the Calhoun contribution is the exploration of theology's essential relation to modern science, and, in particular, to the necessities of modern work. His theology is philosophical, but, even more, *humane.* The theology of Edwin Lewis is dualism; the theology of Robert Calhoun is dynamic monism. Where Nels Ferré is primarily interested in final universal salvation in one or many worlds to come, Calhoun is primarily interested in both personal and social salvation in the midst of the struggle of this world. Where Reinhold Niebuhr is critical of the pride and pretense of human achievement, Calhoun is hopeful that work and worship can be constructively united. Where Paul Tillich is, in appearance, Docetic and abstract, Calhoun is concrete and practical, and in late years Calhoun has moved toward a new appreciation of the Biblically oriented theology largely ignored in Tillich's philosophical preoccupation. Calhoun and Richard Niebuhr are not far apart; both are filled with hope; both are primarily interested in the increase of divinity in the dust of history; both seek the universal salvation that embraces and redeems man and culture in the here and now. The difference between them is between a theoretical and a practical approach. Richard Niebuhr looks at the world of culture, man's achievement, from the world of grace, God's Kingdom. Calhoun looks at the Kingdom from the world of culture — the perspective of the common man. To both, God is a working God, a maker, an artist, laboring to complete an unfinished world and an unfinished man. To both, Christ is the transformer of civilization, and eternity is neither against time nor identical with time, nor above time, nor in paradoxical tension with time, but a larger world which includes time. To both, eternity is not a dimension of time, but time a dimension of eternity. A world exists to be completed in the image of God, and man's work toward his own completion is man's true measure. To both, the Kingdom of God is both actuality, for God rules, and possibility, for God is at work to finish his creation.

Christianity and the daily work of the world, the Church, and the proletariat too long have maintained separate residences. They have not been divorced, only alienated. Calhoun is uniquely a mediator, to bring them back together. As a theological marriage broker, he has arranged their reunion in modernity. To him ivory-tower theology is irreverent and irresponsible; reality involves true worship and true work. Calhoun hangs a sign on the universe: "God at Work." He summons men of every race and class, mechanics as well as musicians, plumbers as well as preachers, to roll up their sleeves and sign on with the divine Foreman. The world of God and the work of man groan and travail together in pain awaiting their own completion. The Calhoun theology is both in heaven and " down to earth." He does not bring heaven down, but earth halfway to heaven.

He was born in St. Cloud, Minnesota, December 30, 1896, son of David Thomas and Lida Brooks (Toomer) Calhoun. He received the B.A. (1915) from Carleton College, and the same school gave him the LL.D. (1946). He holds three degrees from Yale: the B.D. (1918), the M.A. (1919), and the Ph.D. (1923). He has received the D.D. from both the University of Chicago (1941) and Oberlin (1944).

Robert Calhoun married Ella Clay Wakeman, December 24, 1923, and there are four children: David Wakeman, Edward Thomas Davidson, Robert Maurice, and Harriet Huddleston. The second child was named for Robert's younger brother, Edward Thomas

Calhoun, M.D., who died in 1927 at twenty-seven years of age. To him, and to a brother-in-law, Alfred Maurice Wakeman, M.D., who died in 1929 at thirty-two years of age, Calhoun dedicated *God and the Common Life* (1935).

Robert Lowry (sometimes spelled Lowrie) Calhoun was instructor in philosophy and education at Carleton, 1921–1923; from 1923–1926, he was an instructor in the history of theology at Yale. He came up, as one of his students expressed it in private conversation, "the hard way." He was assistant professor of historical theology for six years, and associate professor for four. He has been full professor at Yale since 1936.

His special lectures include a series at Yale (1934), Ohio Wesleyan University (1935), Colgate-Rochester Divinity School (1937), Princeton University (1938 and 1943), the Theological Seminary of the Reformed Churches in the United States (1940), the Jewish Theological Seminary of America (1940), the University of Virginia (1941), the Pacific School of Religion (1942), Harvard (1943 and 1944), Vanderbilt University (1944), and the University of Chicago (1947). He is a member of the American Philosophical Association, the American Theological Association, the American Society of Church History, The American Academy of Political and Social Science, Phi Beta Kappa, Delta Sigma Rho, and Book and Bond at Yale. With Nels F. S. Ferré, he is a Congregational contribution to modern theology.

More research per cubic centimeter has been necessary in the Calhoun study than in any other. Unlike the other theologians, with the exception of H. Richard Niebuhr, he seems loath to bring himself to book. Possibly he has intended to be slow to publish, and plenteous in mercy upon his readers. Apparently he has written only when forced to do so, and only in fragments. His articles and essays are legion, his books three: *God and the Common Life, What Is Man?* (1939), and *God and the Day's Work* (1943). *God and the Common Life* describes man and God at work; properly used, it should enable C.I.O. and A.F.L. to receive Christian baptism. Seventeen years after its publication, the book is given the following Calhoun comment in a personal letter:

" The position presented . . . is one that has a good deal in common with what is often called natural theology. It represents only a part, though a sufficiently representative part, of my theological thinking. Actually, even in this relatively early book, the position I tried to maintain was not simply natural theology, but a position in which faith and reason, revelation and the data supplied to sense perception and interpretable by understanding, are kept in suitable balance. . . . At the same time, it must be said that the perspective of my thinking has altered substantially during the past fifteen years, in the direction of a view that gives very much larger place to Biblical and traditional theology."

Next in time is the small but alert book *What Is Man?* published by the Hazen Foundation. The two abstract fields of science and philosophy, on their own terms, are related to the two practical fields, common sense and religion. The four approaches are four necessities, and each is thoroughly examined. At the end you have, not four men, but one man, and the man is taken seriously as God's half-finished handiwork. *God and the Day's Work,* a Y.M.C.A. publication, describes Christian vocation in an unchristian world, but adds little to the earlier books.

For this study the extended debate between Robert L. Calhoun and Henry N. Wieman in *Christendom,* 1936 and 1937, proved of immense help. Wieman attacked the idea that God and mind are in any sense similar. In his view God is the maker of meaning, and mind is the maker of mechanism: no correlation exists between them. Calhoun insisted that God is more than mind, but not wholly other, that God makes mechanism as well as meaning, since the earth, the stars, and the human body are mechanisms. Further, that mind makes meaning as well as mechanism. The debate was no shadowboxing; the divergence was, and remains, real between Wieman's God of evolutionary philosophy, God as a nebulous thing called *interaction,* and Calhoun's God of Christian theology, God as personal, and more. The two men never came together in their debate, though they found, or pretended to find, or attempted to find, common ground. Calhoun ended the series with Christian love:

" God, if unambiguously good, is not simply growth of organic connections, but a discriminating Power of which growth or unification may be thought of as one function, separation as another. . . .

"Shall we suppose that God can only grow? I believe, rather, in the Logos of God, alive through and through, aware and unwavering. In him is growth, but more than growth. In him is life that is also Light. I believe that he is, as growth alone cannot be, Creator of heaven and earth, as well as Saviour of men. . . .

"These beliefs of mine are theology, not primarily faith. When two men differ in theology or religious philosophy, they necessarily differ, more or less, in religion. But if both trust unreservedly the God whose being is 'uncomprehended' by any theology or religion, they have basis for communion in the midst of continuing difference" ("A Final Statement," *Christendom,* spring 1937, pp. 217, 218).

A dozen additional essays, found in a dozen additional places, proved a dozen additional floodlights on Calhoun's comprehensive theology. His *Lectures on the History of Christian Doctrine* (1948), multigraphed in three volumes for private circulation only, cry aloud to be issued by an alert publisher as a text for colleges and seminaries: the treatment of men and movements is faithful yet original. Calhoun is possibly the exception that proves Lao-tse's rule that wise men are never scholars, and scholars are never wise men. No deficiency of scholarship is apparent; rather, a lifetime of patience with primary sources. His address, "The Gospel for This World," in *Making the Gospel Effective* (1945), offers practicing parsons who would serve the present age a pulpit theology that covers the message and uncovers its meaning. Theologians and philosophers will be pleased or irritated, depending on their point of view, by Calhoun's essay, "The History of Philosophy," published in the Hazen Foundation study, *College Reading and Religion* (Yale University Press, 1948, pp. 1–27). The treatment analyzes twenty-three texts on the history of philosophy — from Schwegler to Russell, and from Stöckl to Copleston: eighteen general, five Roman Catholic. From 1893 to 1914 the dominant attitude toward religion was *critical appreciation;* from 1917 to 1939 *active disparagement* prevailed; since 1941 there has been a noticeable return to *critical appreciation.* The diverse treatments of religion may well represent university trends in the same periods. Among the Romanists, Calhoun found either discriminating or undiscriminating advocacy of papal religion. As he sees it, "the tide is coming in once more." He found that superior scholarship and philosophical competence accompany discerning rather than disparaging or uncritical treatments of religion. Another essay was especially helpful: "Theology and the Humanities," in *The Meaning of the Humanities* (Edited by Theodore Meyer Greene, pp. 119–150. Princeton University Press, 1938). Calhoun pleads for an alliance between history, philosophy, and theology on the one hand, and between literature, fine arts, and theology on the other. In procedure he finds theology closer to history and philosophy, in intent closer to literature and the fine arts, but more than any of them directly seeking to move men's wills. Theology, Calhoun believes, concerns the crucial question, "What must I do to be saved?" A discipline approaches theology in the degree to which it approaches the theme "Man Saved by God." Theology is not faith, but the logic of faith; it needs faith to keep its heart, but the humanities to keep its head.

The Calhoun essay on "Plato as Religious Realist," in the book *Religious Realism,* edited by D. C. Macintosh (pp. 195–251. The Macmillan Company, 1931), redresses the balance from philosophy to religion in the Greek thinker. The interpreters often neglect the religious depth, and stress only the philosophical surface, in Platonic thought. To Calhoun, Plato was both devotee and critic of religion, an antinominalist, concerned with the eternal reality of forms, and specifically a theist. In the essay, "Church, State, and Human Devotion," in the symposium *Church and State in the Modern World,* edited by Henry Pitney Van Dusen (pp. 43–82. Harper & Brothers, 1937), Calhoun deals with the problem familiar in Richard Niebuhr's *Christ and Culture.* The Church, ever in danger of uncritical conformity to the State, must bear witness to a reality greater than Church and State. On Calhoun's terms, God is the ultimate term in man's environment, transcendent beyond every fact and form. To identify him with the human community, or his will with government policy, is absurd. A needed word for educators, whether public or private, is found in Calhoun's essay, "The Place of Religion in Higher Education," in the book *Religion and the Modern World* (Pp. 63–70. University of Pennsylvania Press, 1941). Calhoun understands that civilized living is possible only for people at once disciplined and free: to this end three things are necessary — specialized skills, specialized knowledge, and a perspective or unifying frame. Thus high religion and intellectual enterprise belong together. Each has something to give, something to gain. Both are stronger together than apart.

Men concerned with Christian conscience in a world at war will find more light than heat in the report of the Federal Council Commission on the Relation of the Church to the War in the Light of the Christian Faith. Calhoun was final editor of the report, and chairman of the Commission that prepared it. John C. Bennett was Commission secretary; Edwin E. Aubrey, Roland H. Bainton, and H. Richard Niebuhr were responsible for empirical, historical, and theological subsections. Calhoun, Bennett, and John Knox made the final revisions; and the study, in significant part, was published in *Social Action,* December 15, 1944. The report contains both mature theology and practical counsel for the Church and the Christian in wartime. The document, like the *kairos* theology of Tillich, urges that the Christian revelation and the contemporary situation must both be understood. War is an event in the providential reign of God, whom we know best through the crucified and triumphant Christ. For Christian faith the cataclysm of war is a tragic movement in God's work of creating and redeeming man, and in man's long struggle with himself and his Creator. Man is a sinner, but salvable, both individually and institutionally. Hence, war can be abolished. Tension in the Church is inevitable: its members are divinely required to aid and abet their governments, and at the same time to take the Church seriously as an ecumenical society, transcending all governments. The Church is literally on both sides of every war: it is with its people as their minister, where they are and as they are; yet it is also one community, one communion, across all national barriers. Its own unity must increase, that the world's disunity may decrease. Our interlocked society must be transformed into world community, that great nations may play contributive rather than destructive roles. A free international community must be built, without paternalism or servitude, in spite of the fact that freedom is decreased and disunity increased by modern total war. The Church must oppose unfalteringly the calculated ruthlessness of war, yet take into account its own divided loyalty, human weakness, and secular involvement. The primary ground for a distinctive Christian understanding of any situation is the revelation of God in Jesus Christ; in this understanding the New Testament and the Church are inseparable.

An important work in systematic theology is on the way. In February, 1952, Calhoun delivered four addresses for the Yale University Christian Mission, and transcripts were made from tape recordings. These fragments are parts of a body of material in process of development over a considerable period of time. When complete, the project may be issued as a text in systematics, and should prove a major publishing event.

Genuine humility, patient accuracy, and profound insight characterize every Calhoun paragraph. His approach is always broadly, not narrowly, behavioristic; he warns the reader against the prejudices of his Western masculine viewpoint, and against his layman's lack of competence in technical fields. Upon investigation, his technical competence needs no apology, and is always wedded to depth and breadth of meaning. He reunites practical and speculative thought, and examines boldly both the oldest, homeliest practice and the newest far-flung theory.

Dean L. A. Weigle and Professor J. E. Boodin, Calhoun acknowledges, introduced him to undergraduate philosophy. Professors A. K. Rogers and C. A. A. Bennett furthered his philosophical development, and D. C. Macintosh awakened his interest in theology. He acquired the scientific method and spirit, and a firsthand acquaintance with the natural sciences, from Professors F. F. Exner, L. A. Headley, R. S. Lull, Raymond Hussey "chiefly through my brother," Clark Hull, and Dr. A. J. Wakeman. From two young medical men, Edward Thomas Calhoun and Alfred Maurice Wakeman, close to him in love and memory, Calhoun believes that he has learned, in scientific matters, most of all.

Colleagues, he confesses, have helped him immeasurably. Among them are: Roland Bainton, Richard and Reinhold Niebuhr, Cornelius Krusé, Filmer Northrop, Edwin Aubrey, John Bennett, Herman Brautigam, and John K. Benton. "A small ungloved, tough-minded circle called 'the Club'" widened Calhoun's horizons. Twenty-six "assorted and strenuous" companions saved him from premature maturity. We have met this discussion group in our study of Tillich. A. N. Whitehead's later writings proved a kind of revelation.

Calhoun ranks high one influence often underestimated:

" The household in which Ella Wakeman Calhoun, and David, Ted, Robert Maurice, Harriet, and I have lived together at close range has done more to my thinking than any of them suspects. It is these, with my mother while she lived, who have made it seem to me intolerable to think and write theology without continual reference to everyday needs and facts " (*God and the Common Life,* p. xi. Charles Scribner's Sons, 1935).

MAN — PRODUCT AND PARTICIPANT

Man and his world are in the making; no resting place is final; the end is not yet. God is precisely *at work*. Herein lies our anguish and our hope. Calhoun begins and ends with this idea.

Ground-clearing operations were completed before we were born, before Christianity was born. Judaism worshiped, and now worships, a God high and lifted up, whose law is love. Neither Babylon, Greece, nor Rome could induce the Jews to bow down before man-made gods, and modern paganism has not been more successful. In this moral and virile faith Christianity was born. In its youth, it was powerful enough to incorporate and transfigure Hellenism, the mystery cults, and Roman discipline. The backbone of Christianity was, and remains, Hebrew monotheism and Hebrew morale vitally embodied in Jesus of Nazareth. In him a plain fisherman saw the Christ, the Son of the living God; from this belief came the conviction of Pentecost that in him men had seen God face to face.

Christianity, the end of preparatory religion, increased both Jewish pessimism and Jewish optimism. When the two are separated, world hatred or world idolatry results. Together they form the powerful Christian counterpoint of desperation and hope.

Christian pessimism sees man as he is; Christian optimism sees God as he is. Pessimism, which takes seriously the plight of man, understands that intellectual and moral education does not get to the root of the trouble. Man's problem is centered in his feelings and desires, beneath the level of conscious thought and will. A man is what he *loves*. Man is a mass of misdirected cravings: he possesses a " second nature " of acquired depravity; he cannot choose as he ought; he cannot, by willful effort, fulfill the law of God. In Calhoun's words:

" There is no need to exaggerate. Nor is there any need to leave the firm ground of experience and the familiar atmosphere of modern thought to see what the Christian analysis of man's plight has in view. It has its eyes on man the animal, as we know him in business, in politics, and in war; in the hypocrisies of home and school and church, and all polite society; in the secret lusts and hates of his most private imaginings, and in the waking nightmares of his madness when these lusts and hates come out frankly, inside hospital cells or in lynchings and pogroms. Who indeed shall deliver man, ourselves and our fellow animals, from the body of this death?

" Not high ideals and moral discourses. Not common sense, nor science, nor philosophy. They can all help, but not enough. And above all, not the cults of race and class that sanctify hatred and lust, seeking to free man from conscience and the claims of *right* by handing him over to the whirlwinds of raw *power*. Man is an animal, predatory, deceitful, cruel. But he is no less incurably a social, responsible, aspiring animal, who can no more rid himself of conscience than of his memory or his powers of speech, without ceasing to be a man " (*What Is Man?*, p. 70. Association Press, 1939).

Man the world child seeks animal escape from world responsibility: he adopts Nazi tribalism or Communist dynamism. But drugs wear off. Human nerves can stand just so much marching and shouting and regimented cruelty. Then comes nausea, and the cold, drab light; men temporarily gone animal have to face once more the fact that they are men, with the problem that is man still unsolved.

Man is precisely the question, " What is man? " The question is not theoretical at all, but fearfully practical: " *What must I be and do to be human?* " The answer is not, " Go on as you are." The answer is not in man, but in the power and goodness of God. Our only hope is that God in some sense loves us powerfully enough to rescue us from our own ambiguity. Just this is the affirmation of Christian faith. " God so *loved*."

Nobody knows literally how God, the Creator and Lord of a universe measured in light-years, could have an " only Son " on earth; nobody knows how God himself could come in human form to save men from themselves. Nonetheless the language of myth expresses a faith that has thrived on suffering, a hope and a love that have heartened men through dark centuries of struggle. The fact remains that, with the coming of Jesus as the Christ, redeeming energy was liberated among men. That renewing power has made headway against overwhelming obstacles, bettered millions of lives, and dredged deep channels through history. This is not to say that men were not saved before Jesus appeared. It is to say that never before did this saving power manifest itself with equal effect, that the turning point in human life has been reached. Personal trust in the transforming power of God, made flesh in Jesus Christ, is Christian faith. The transforming power of God, at work in this world, is the ground of Christian hope. The blackest pessimism concerning man is thus transcended. The Christian's hope for men is inexhaustible because his hope is not in men; he believes that God *is,* and that he is Creator, Father, and Saviour. Yet in all religious affirmation there remains a basic venture, an inescapable risk. But one thing is sure. The Christian understanding of man, including both relentless pessimism and exultant faith, offers no ordinary utopia; it goes deeper than dream; it sees man not merely rehoused and re-educated, but remade. It does not crudely glorify man, but sees him, even at his worst, as never alone but always surrounded with God. In the divine presence man lives, and moves, and has his being. God holds man in his hand. If hope exists for man the animal, stresses Calhoun, it is because something like this is true. Because God is a Man of Work, it does not yet appear what we shall be. We are less than gods, and more than historians; both actuality and possibility possess us.

Calhoun's own faith illustrates both the precariousness and the predictability of the Christian venture. He writes: " My own belief in God, and I suspect that of many others who believe, has been generated painfully enough, not by argument but by the concrete ebb and flow of living, in ways that I do not fully understand and cannot control " (*God and the Common Life,* p. 3). Man in the making moves forward by steadiness and by riskiness through a world in the making toward the unfinished City of God. Man and world are in motion together, like sailor and ship upon troubled seas. The believer realizes that he can neither fully understand the Master's purpose nor fail to trust it. In clear weather our more expert human navigators would chart a truer course by the stars. But at the moment the experts are having difficulties of their own. We plain mariners must find our way by compass and dead reckoning, that is, without celestial observation. Man is ambiguous; even nature is not clear. Within our own generation nature has ceased to speak the plain, downright, British English of Newton and Darwin, as five hundred years ago she abandoned the dry, lucid Latin of Aquinas on Aristotle. The best we can do is to gain what Cusanus called "instructed ignorance" (*docta ignorantia*), the complicated tentativeness of those who expertly know that they know not, and somewhat expertly why.

The prime concern of theology, Calhoun insists, is to help men to keep rightly oriented in the midst of actual living. Neither abstract principles nor detailed techniques are outside the theologian's domain. However, he must devote himself, as a specialist, neither to the one nor to the other. He must try to see how facts and principles illumine one another. Where relevant data are inaccessible, where specialists do not agree as to what is open for inspection, exactitude is not to be had. In any case, something more is needed than evolution, the idol of liberalism, and something more as well than disillusion, the idol of Marxian and Barthian reaction. We need more than stars and stout shipmates; we need some idea of direction.

Modern man's place to begin, after all, is the day's work and the yearly round. By nature and of right God and work belong together, for man is product of the past and participant in the present. Secularized weekdays and formalized Sabbaths are scarred fragments; neither separately nor together is there life in them. If we are to be more than *hypocritai,* play actors, we must be more than spiritual starvelings; we need stronger food than discriminating words, thoughts, misgivings, and regrets; we need heavier exercise than diffident reform. Our Protestant grandsires, with their sinewy piety, knew plenty of restraints, but nothing of thin-blooded diffidence.

Without positive, concrete convictions there can be no effective sense of day-to-day urgency, opportunity, and obligation. In simple zeal the thinner sorts of Christianity do not compare favorably with youthful Communism.

Work is required of man, because God is a worker. Against the monastic ideal, that monks were more pleasing to God than ordinary folk doing the ordinary work of the world, Luther and Calvin applied to these common pursuits the impressive term *vocatio*, " divine calling." A few mystics had roundly asserted that the highest level of perfection was possible not only for the monk but equally for the humblest laborer — the man flailing corn or braking nettles: any earthly occupation wherein one toiled faithfully and lovingly in the service of his neighbor could be a medium for the vision of God — yet in Tauler's view, contemplation was higher than action. The Reformers took a further drastic step: they extended the call of God from saints to sinners, from Church to world. On their terms, monastic austerities for excess merit were worse than useless; only through faithfulness in the appointed daily task was obedience acceptable to God. Luther, Calvin, and their contemporaries created a genuinely new estimate of everyday life and work. It was freshly understood that the adoration of God included daily toil. But Luther, Calvin, and their heirs were primarily interested in ecclesiastical reform, not in social reconstruction. They were economically naïve and politically conservative. Neither was willing to concede man's ability to find salvation in this world. Lutheran quietism and Calvinist asceticism alike ignored social economics. In New England, for a time, daily work was rightly understood as divine vocation, something more than a theological abstraction. The plain man was not disobedient to the heavenly vision as he went from meetinghouse or chapel to carry on the daily round. Once again, God was served through common toil. But the individualism of the Puritan, accompanied by his toil, in time created capitalism. The poetry of earthly divine calling cooled into middle-class prose. Vocation secularized was vocation emasculated. Give was replaced by grab. Proud nationalism and economic imperialism flexed their muscles round the world. As Weber understood in 1905, specialists without spirit and sensualists without soul — this nullity imagines it has attained the highest level of civilization. Secularism has created the abomination of desolation. Calhoun describes the capitalist spiritual vacuum thus:

" Machine tools that finally insured the triumph of middle-class capitalism have now mechanized the lives of all but a privileged few who live within its sway. Most of those who work are slaves now to subways and steam whistles; and these leave less marginal energy and freedom for savoring the present, and dwelling on the future, than even field laborers had in the old regime. Moreover, the part of the ordinary worker in much of modern industry and trade has been trivialized to the point of boredom and preclusion of self-respect. Snipping endlessly the pieces of cheap cloth for shoddy garments; punching endlessly the paper and split leather soles for bargain shoes; feeding endlessly the rods, wire, and sheet metal that become ten-cent hardware; selling endlessly cheap merchandise in a cheap market; finding romance in cheap movies and wood-pulp magazines. Who is fool enough to look for God, even if one were sure there is a God, in this dreary modern warehouse? " (*Ibid.,* p. 30).

It is time for a new beginning. No one-sided return to Calvin or Luther or Paul will suffice. They lived by vocation, as holy men, but their doctrine of vocation was inadequate. They were flame-touched insurgents who lived beyond their doctrine. Their lives demonstrated that commitment to things as they are, in an imperfect world, is the death of moral and religious aspiration, yet that contempt for the world as it is keeps aspiration unsullied but cuts the nerve of action. The Voice in our own day commands us to go forward in the name of God.

All men are called to become fully human, to work in a world unfinished, full of unexplored resources and demands. The first requirement of divine vocation is that our work be needful: this is our general calling. The second requirement is that our work fulfill our need to work, that our work be fitted to our powers: this is our special calling. The third requirement is that we accept our full contributive share in the world's work and the common life. We are called to live, not our neighbor's or our nation's or our church's life, but our own, yet we must lose our lives to find them, even in work. For most of us the carpenter shop precedes the cross, and it is required that we be faithful over a few things. As Calhoun puts it:

" To do needful work, then; to lose oneself and find oneself therein; to participate thus in a common task and a shared life: this, and the summons to it, we shall mean by vocation, which may serve to guide in part a serious effort to live in the world as it is and toward a world as it ought to be. . . . While steadily refusing to look for a Kingdom of Heaven on earth, past, present, or to come, in which men would be gods and life one grand sweet song, we steadily hope for a time when more men can be more fully men. . . . Our hope is first of all in what the world order may portend: that order which with silent condemnation and promise calls mankind back, again and again, from the bogs of unbridled competitive war to the road of contributive work. Not dogmatically, but quite soberly . . . we regard that call as coming ultimately not from men, nor from dialectically moving matter, but from God " (*Ibid.*, p. 71).

In simplest terms, there is in everything and in every man a yawning discrepancy between what ought to be and what is. Come to terms with this world, with all its discrepancies, we must, or go mad; but acquiesce we may not, and keep morally sane. Religious realism is neither final pessimism nor final optimism; it is convinced that the actual ought to be, and can be, changed for the better. The crucial line between better and worse cuts not *between* sacred and secular groups, the elected and the rejected, the saved and the damned, but through every occupation, every group, and every life. The unambiguous ideal has always an ambiguous relation to this world: it is pertinent to and partly exemplified by, but neither identical with nor completely present in, any actual thing or event. Man leans and sometimes lifts, but he lifts most and leans least when he realizes that he himself is lifted, and called to lift by a weight-lifting God. When competence becomes technical mastery, and conscious responsibility becomes intense love for one's work, the workman is an artist, in the basic meaning of the word. For every man at every moment the tension between what is and what ought to be cannot be relaxed. Perfection is not to be looked for here, but we must refuse to acquiesce in the finality of anything less.

The human mind is both immanent in, and transcendent over, every present situation. It is immanent in so far as it enters into direct causal and stimulus-response relations with what is actually here.

It transcends the immediate situation in so far as, by way of symbolic behavior, it takes account also of what is not actually here. Man is therefore *product,* a world child, and *problem,* a world project. It is his glory that he may become in some degree a *participant* in the world process.

A Working God

Calhoun paints his portrait of God the Worker with Thomas Aquinas' " principle of sufficient reason ": from the existence and order of the world as perceptible and intelligible, it is permissible to argue to the existence and actuality of a Being sufficient to account for the facts observed. If you saw a large field slowly filling with piles of brick, bags of cement, stacks of lumber, and steel construction equipment, with trucks and bulldozers roaring to and fro, with gangs of men at work on foundations, and other men with blueprints surveying the scene, consulting, measuring, directing, you would certainly conclude that somewhere a mind was at work with a purpose, that a school or office building would shortly appear. Endless preplanning, prefiguring, and rearranging are inevitable in such an undertaking — all evidences of purposive, or mental, activity. Similarly Calhoun argues from the evidence of the natural and historical process to ultimate Mind, the cosmic Designer or Contractor or Creator. Our universe, like the large field filled with building materials, is in process. The completed structure does not yet appear, and only a fraction of the blueprint. One step is enough for us. Sufficient unto every day is the work thereof. Man is product, problem, and participant in God's unfinished world. Flux and form are always present: at every moment the world has the look of perpetual incompleteness and partly ordered becoming. God is at work. " My Father worketh even until now," said Jesus, " and I work."

Persons, whether divine or human, can reveal themselves to other persons only through their works — whether words or deeds; here also the principle of sufficient reason operates. We know God and each other only through our works; we argue from the existence and order of events as perceptible and intelligible to the existence and activity of persons sufficient to account for the events experienced.

God works even until now, and we work. The world is not yet fully made, nor wholly good; and at the present, whatever may have been true in the prehistoric past, other factors than God are also at work. But God is primary, central, and sovereign over all. World-making is the meaning of creation and redemption: God's Kingdom is both actuality and possibility. As Calhoun sees it, God's relation to the actual world is like my relation to my own life — not my body merely, but the total of my experience. At one and the same moment, I am immanent in my experience and transcendent over it; thus God is both transcendent over his experience, which includes our world, and is immanent within it. He is thus omnipresent in the total process, as I am omnipresent in my total life. No event is hidden from him. His apprehension encompasses all that has transpired and is transpiring in the total time span. Through his transcendence he has access as well to all that *can* happen. Like us, God is Subject, known through his activity; and, like us, God cannot know in full what has not yet come to pass. His foreknowledge is not complete, and this means not deficiency but definiteness. Omnipresent throughout the world order, though not of it nor encompassed within it, he is everywhere near. His knowledge, like ours, is selective. God's mind is not occupied impartially with relevant and irrelevant possibilities, ad infinitum. There is a world in the making. God is occupied with specific problems, that is, he works upon us, not according to our wishes, but according to our needs.

God is Omnipotent Doer as well as Omnipresent Knower. He acts to realize the good, the Kingdom of what ought to be. This is the center of religious faith. The world is great: that needs no proof. The sovereign power is good: this admits no proof. But to affirm it with all the mind and heart is to believe in God, great beyond our conceiving, yet not too great to be good. God is not hampered by our limitations: ignorance, inner conflict, space-time restriction, inferiority to particular finite forces. And he is no more bound by past behavior patterns than is a skilled physician by the memorandum he has made at an earlier stage in a patient's illness. Unlike us,, God's conflicts are with the world, not with himself. His work can be hindered, but not defeated. Yet the divine omnipotence is not absolute: his power is limited by his nature — his wisdom, justice, and mercy. Perfection involves limitation, that is, inner harmony and balance, not indiscriminate and infinite aggregation. God is not only limited by his own intrinsic nature, which cannot act otherwise than to realize the good, but he is also limited by certain external rigidities, not evil but good elements which contribute to constructive work. God cannot build a fifty-foot house on a forty-foot lot; though he can and does turn evil into good, he cannot reverse the actual series of events — that is, the future is not actually present. God is limited also by the social rigidities: inertia and fatigue. For God as well as for men, in Calhoun's judgment, these hindrances have to be transcended; at no actual point in the world process are they completely eliminated. God is limited also by the fluence of flux, the crude movement of the process, the real contingency and indeterminacy of events. No event is rigorously determined until it happens. As Plato understood, God, and with God chance and contingency, governs human affairs. Every concrete individual, from electron to quanta, and from amoeba to man, has a certain waywardness: none is fully amenable to God's will. Finite persons can and do oppose their wills to one another and to God. God's radical transcendence means that he is wholly other, as we are wholly other to each other, yet his transcendence is relative and not absolute. Love in God, however far beyond anything I know, has something in common with love in me; and so with power, justice, and joy. Herein lies the reasonableness of the command, " Be ye perfect, even as your Father which is in heaven is perfect." And God's immanence is communicative: by revelation and inspiration he makes himself known to us and quickens us into life. God's very refusal to be what I want him to be can draw me nearer to that which he is. Our relation to God is the relation of subject to Subject, yet between God and the self a more intimate relationship can exist than between one self and another. In Calhoun's words:

" God . . . , by revealing himself to men, awakens in them responses that well up from the deeper springs within them. But these deep springs themselves have been called into being by the God who now arouses them to action. . . . The goal . . . toward which a God-quickened man

finds himself newly oriented may be called either the good, or God. . . .
The good is not more than God. . . . If we say, then, that the Spirit of
God comes upon men, and that they are filled with the Holy Spirit, we
should mean, I think, that by the perpetual summons of God, which
comes through the whole natural and social network within which God
and men are continuously side by side and face to face, men are quick-
ened now and again to respond on new higher and deeper levels " (*Ibid.,*
p. 200).

The way of man with God is work and worship; the two must not
be separated, yet are not identical. Human extremity is worship's
most poignant occasion, and repentance and moral regeneration
worship's meaning. In true worship, a man recognizes that the
source of dislocation is in himself, that the thwarting of his hopes
is not only deserved and necessary but to be welcomed. Worship is
more than appreciation; it is the venture of self-commitment, the
cautious recklessness of God.

The way of God with man involves communication, co-working,
and transcendent sovereignty. Words may point toward God, but
cannot make him known. He makes himself known as Mind, Spirit,
Holy Will at work within and upon our half-made actual world.
Men are not parts of God, nor one with God, nor gods in their own
right. They are selves who may become sons, colaborers with God
in the task of world-making. Man is called to be a contributing participant in the shared task and the common life. The call is not
coercive: each man's response is his own. But the initiative is first
and forever God's. The starry heavens above and the moral law
within offer general revelation; illuminating crises, disturbing but
driving forward the stream of events, offer special revelation. Jesus'
life and death is not self-explanatory: the meaning exists for faith,
insight, and devotion. God is both discontinuous and continuous
with man and the world: the world is God's but not God. There are
real problems — for God as well as for man.

Calhoun's humility is sincere. He understands that we must tell
our stories of God as best we can, and know when we have finished
that silence is better. Nonetheless, we must act on the basis of our
beliefs. Our basic conviction, as Calhoun sees it, is this:

"Christianity, at its best, has both depth and breadth — and height. Its primary trust is neither in individual men nor in social groups, nor in mankind, but in the God and Father revealed in Jesus Christ. The one true God is universal sovereign. He is not a tribal deity; neither is he merely an indwelling, evolutionary urge, nor a humanly conceived ideal. He is a transcendent God, and therefore has authority for all mankind. . . .

"We are asking that the essential Christian gospel may once more come into our world with life-transforming power. . . . The story is not the decorous children's tale told in churches at Christmas and Easter; it is the gospel that once moved with power through the mighty Roman Empire and unseated its ancient gods. . . . The inmost core of life, strong and sweet and caustic as flame, has been in that story" (*God and the Day's Work*, pp. 3, 6. Association Press, 1943).

True religion calls forth a person's entire range of capacities and skills into worship and devoted work for the common good; the Power that calls is not only greater than man but greater also than the earth and the stars.

A Working Gospel

Many advocates of the gospel in our time accent its usefulness for public morals or morale, its value as insurance against eternal or even temporal loss. All such advocacy of the gospel, in Calhoun's opinion, misses the point. Anyone who seeks to make use of religious faith for political or economic advantage misconceives it. Nonetheless, the gospel is an invaluable resource, a power for full-scale living. To the eye of faith, our time, like every other, is marked with guidelines for thought and action, and the present is charged with eternal promise.

Since the gospel is permanent and universal, it can afford to speak to every time in its own tongue. The ancient gospel looks well in modern dress. The divine sovereignty is always present tense.

The preaching of the gospel in this age, thinks Calhoun, must stress three things: the necessity of repentance in view of the reality of sin; the good ground that exists for hope; and the unavoidable demand for righteousness, at once impossible and imperative.

In recent years the sinner as helpless victim has held the center of attention, and the emphasis in part was long overdue: it cleared away some of the vindictiveness of the saints from the Inquisition in Spain to witch-burning in New England or Negro-lynching in the South. But the " helpless victim " idea has been overemphasized, for the sinner is cause as well as effect. By definition sin involves responsibility. Where there is no responsibility, there is no sin. The gospel neither condemns nor coddles the sinner.

A good doctor, in his struggle against disease, neither condemns nor coddles his patient. Something of the same precision and patience, not wholly unlike the aim and attitude of the Good Physician, has long been needed in our dealing with personal and social sin. Nonetheless, sin is still sin, and the concept is indispensable. Sin is wrongdoing, not misfortune. Sin, unlike misfortune, is personal decision, self-commitment, active self-identification with what is wrong. Sin is therefore more than antisocial: it is anti-God; it is perversion of personal existence, not natural disaster. In war and in peace, in every human enterprise, in every human life, in every response to the natural and human environment, there is sin.

The source of sin is unfaith, that is, lack of trust in God and man, the fear and the falsehood called anxiety. The devil is indeed the father of lies. Sin is both individual and corporate, though group sin is ambiguous: not every member of the sinful group is personally committed to its sin. Because responsible individuals participate, the group becomes a seedbed of sin.

Because sin is a reality, repentance is a necessity. True preaching can neglect neither the one nor the other. Repentance is called for individually and socially, in class, race, country, and coalition. Repentance is an absolute essential in all healthy human living: it is not morbid and inverted self-righteousness. Doleful egoism is not penitence. Genuine repentance has an objective reference: it is a recovery of perspective, a reorientation of aim; clear thinking and active decision, not feeling, are primary. The healthy soul rejects wrong, once it is seen to be wrong, as a healthy body rejects poison. Repentance that is more than a mild glow of virtuousness begins most often in moral frustration. A man discovers that the fault lies within, not outside, his struggling will. He recognizes an inner distortion, which can be corrected neither by exertion nor by change of fortune. In oneself, not elsewhere, is the blame. The badly set bone must be rebroken to grow straight. Repentance is not just being sorry; it is the drastic resetting of a crooked life. True repentance is a gift of God: to the blind light must be given — it cannot be grasped. To see ourselves as God sees us is to be illumined by his Spirit.

The crucial decision — to accept and follow the new light — is a man's response to God's redemptive summons. Repentance is easier for individuals than for groups: groups are afflicted, more than individuals, with self-righteousness. Group laws are always the laws of the Medes and the Persians which cannot be changed: they are inflexible in operation and infallible in assumption. Health in the nations, united or separated, more obviously than in individuals, is a divine gift: the initiative of necessity comes from God, first through the critic, and when the critic is ignored, through judgment, the dead-end street of false absolutes.

Sin and repentance are realities, but real also is the ground of our hope. There is hope both in man and in God: in every situation human strength exalts itself against divine order, and in the strength, as well as in the order, the better is promised. Human strength is good, though misdirected; there is always hope of its redirection. Human energy of mind and hand achieves greatly when one in will with God. Secondly, there is real hope for man in God's historical self-disclosure. One God and one man made one Christ; one God and one mankind make one Kingdom. God has accomplished much in history, with or without the pessimists' permission: there is irreversible movement, and it is always forward, though sometimes through strategic retreat. Control over the material conditions of life is clearly on the increase; the promise is real that within a hundred years men everywhere may be freed from famine, from futility in toil, and from the false grandeur and factual misery of the caste system. Technological progress is not moral progress, not a substitute for the Kingdom of God: as man's master it is his enemy; as his servant, his friend. Technology, on Toynbee's terms, has made of many pasts one economic present; two tasks remain — to build one political and one religious future.

There is hope in mankind's long-demonstrated toughness and

adaptability. Mankind's survival through a thousand centuries of bloodshed is miracle enough for ecstatic faith. The farther back biologists push mankind's beginning, the greater the miracle. How come man has not perished of his own stupidity? There is more to man than meets the eye: his very longevity is ground for hope. To the man who adds meaning to measurement, human survival is the evidence of present salvation, and the assurance of future completion; toughness and adaptability are not original achievements but original gifts, not cause, but result. Even our present woes are evidence, not of futile weakness, but of fearful strength.

God was here before we were; God is stronger than we are; his concern is greater than our own. This is our ultimate hope — that God is God. Our moral failures are understandable and curable, not chaotic. This world, on any account, necessitates physical and moral learning: It is God's educational institution to teach us both liberal and mechanical arts; it is God's schoolmaster to bring us to ourselves, to himself, and to one another. God speaks in the total process, but most clearly in Jesus Christ and his Church. Our knowledge is not an end, but an instrument — to bring men to God and Love to men. Jesus Christ and his Church, Head and body together, present in history the purpose of history. His life was, and remains, the end of the beginning, and the beginning of the end, in man-making. In Jesus Christ and his Church the ground was broken for the building of the commonwealth of God. The creation, the redemption, as Augustine affirmed, began with human history, was revealed in Christ and his Church, has continued without a break to this moment, and will continue to and through the millennium. Herein is still man's hope. In human flesh has been revealed the power, truth, and love against which human wickedness and physical disaster are powerless.

The working gospel involves not only the reality of sin and the necessity of repentance, not only the real ground for hope, but also the endless anguish of absolute demand. The gospel is both *imperative* and *impossible*. The absolute demand is not a set of rules but a set of soul. "Be ye perfect," said Christ. We can neither fulfill nor evade the demand. Our best intelligence and integrity are required:

at every moment we must accept, and reject, ourselves as we are and our world as it is. By faith and hope and love we are to move at every moment with the Church Godward, and with God worldward. With unstinting generosity in thought and action we are to acknowledge each day the complex excellence and the incompleteness of all human behavior, including our own. Callous or cruel action reacts promptly upon our own character; generosity and forgiveness do likewise. In very truth life is measured to us with the same measure we ourselves use. As we give, so we receive. God's justice is not for its own sake but for our sake; it is never vindictive; it is always creative and gracious; for this reason we call God Father. In Calhoun's words:

" Our gospel . . . begins and ends with imperatives that are grounded in the nature of man and the presence of God. It centers in the revelation of God in human history, especially in Jesus Christ crucified and the community of grace that widens around him. The God who has given himself and his Son thus freely has not yet failed those who trust him. He will not fail us in the hard years ahead " (" The Gospel for This World," in *Making the Gospel Effective,* ed. by William K. Anderson, p. 34. Nashville, Methodist Commission on Ministerial Training, 1945).

We live in a century of war. As Calhoun sees it, war is neither simply a natural fact nor an act of God nor a sinful choice of man. It is a complex event in which all these factors are present and need to be recognized. In every war, God is not neutral and he is not helpless. He is maintaining invincibly an order that men cannot overthrow. Moreover, he is taking sides through the struggle, not with Communist or capitalist powers or with the United Nations, not with any church or with any churchman, but with the impulse toward good, and against the impulse toward evil, in every man and every movement at every moment. God is not a combatant, nor a neutral onlooker, nor a helpless victim. In war as in peace he is the Creator and Sovereign whose power sustains and governs, but does not annul, the activities of nature and of men.

War is overcome in principle only in the Church, for the Church is the union of God and man. Because God is God, and God is just-judging Love, the Church is the Gunga Din on both sides of every conflict, minister to all men — the critic and the servant of oppressor and oppressed. The task of the Church is reconciliation, between man and God, between man and man, and between the present and the future. The Church is not a partner of any state, but the conscience of every state. It is the organ of hope, the nucleus of world community; its business is not to rule, but to heal. In Calhoun's words:

" The Church that began as a handful of unknown disciples has grown, tenaciously and irrepressibly, through the centuries. Its breadth now, around the globe, is undergirded with the depth and power of proved vitality. . . .

" Within its walls, men of all races and cultures have their rightful homes. It will need to make their claims to brotherhood more evident and effective. . . .

" With all its faults, the Christian Church in our time is an actual massive embodiment of growing community, and the only one whose organized membership is world-wide. . . .

" The Church . . . with its faith grounded in the Everliving God, whose Spirit moves still within his half-finished creation, can by its very existence as faithful Church help the world to find the way. The Church must seek to realize yet more fully its own growing unity of spirit, to bring into its communion of faith and love an even more inclusive company of God's children, and to make its own awareness of divine judgment and forgiveness pervade, like widening daylight, the whole tortured life of our time" (*Social Action*, Vol. X, No. 10, December 15, 1944, pp. 77, 78).